P

# GUIDE TO MAKING WOODEN TOYS THAT MOVE

POPULAR CRAFTS

# GUIDE TO MAKING WOODEN TOYS THAT MOVE

ALAN & GILL BRIDGEWATER

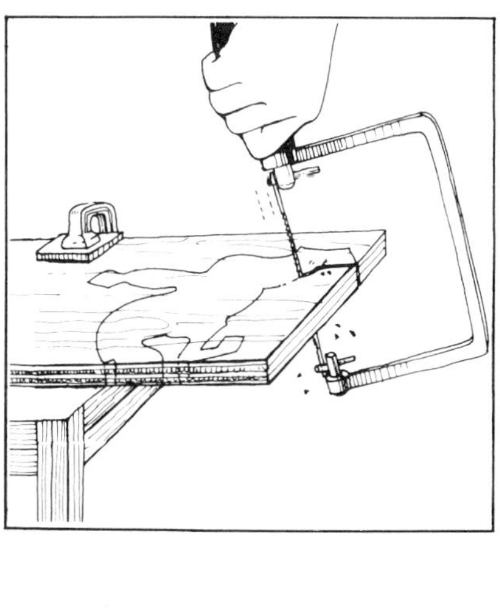

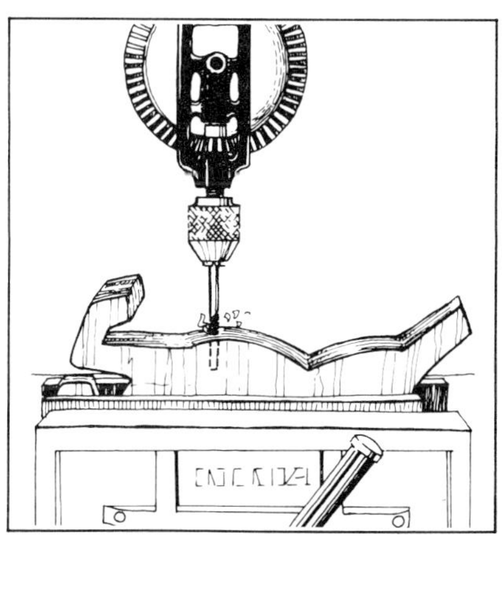

ARGUS BOOKS LIMITED

Argus Books Limited
1 Golden Square
London W1R 3AB



ISBN 0 85242 863 4



Phototypesetting by En to En, Tunbridge Wells
Printed and bound by R. J. Acford, Chichester

# PREFACE

Welcome to the world of wooden moving toys. Welcome to a world of shiny sharpe edge tools, beautiful sweet smelling woods, crinkly tracing papers and bright flowing paints. The ambitions of this book are simple; we just want you to have lots of pleasure designing and making one or other of our little toys.

When we initially sat down and thought this book out, we tried to picture in our mind's eye you the reader. We pondered and puzzled — are you old? Are you male or female? Are you an experienced crafts person? Do you want to set yourself up as a toymaker? Are you a young mum looking for a profitable hobby? Are you a grandparent who just wants to make a special one-off toy for a grandchild? We spent many a long evening with pencils and paper desperately trying to analyse our reader market. Well of course, we eventually came to the conclusion that you are no more or less, than our friend, our neighbour — that is to say, you are a kindred spirit who just wants to enjoy and experience the pleasures of creation. To take a piece of wood and a few scraps of this and that, and to make say a horse that swings and sways, or a little gymnast that does the most amazing topsy turvy stunts; simple pleasures maybe, but they take a bit of beating.

When we first started making these toys, what a laugh! — my wife Gill broke half a dozen saw blades before she got the hang of the coping saw, and my two boys were up to their armpits in glue and paint; I'm sure you can picture the scene. But when we had our first little toy all set up and working, what a feeling! We had made it, and we had turned all those bits of wood into

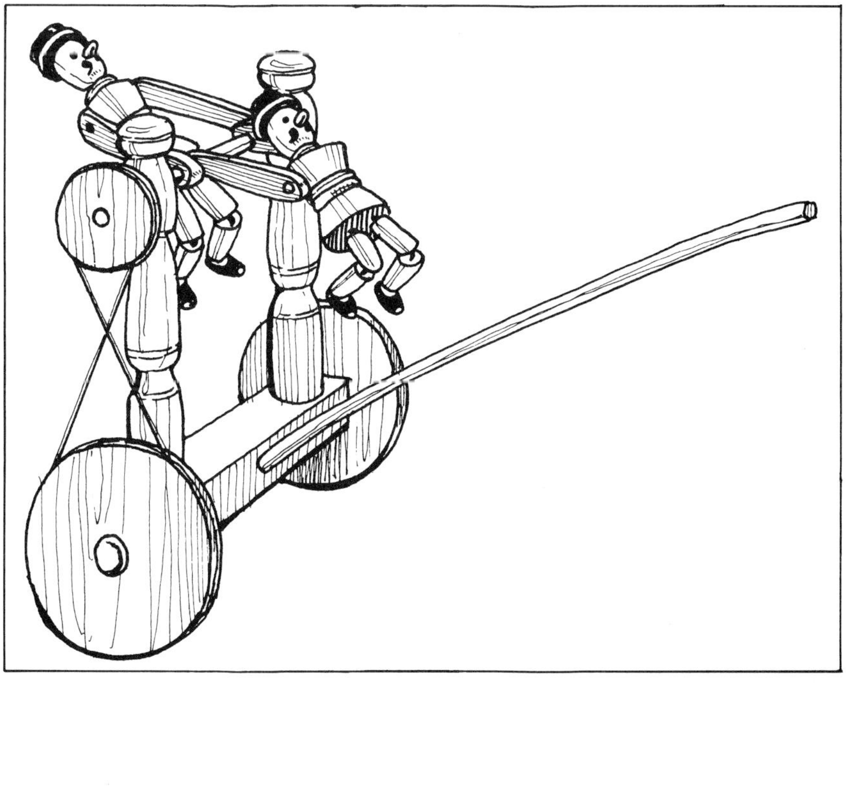

something that seemed to move of its own accord. And of course it didn't stop there; soon friends and relations, inspired by our enthusiasm, were bringing us books on traditional folk toys, and even bringing us old toys that they had spotted at jumble sales and junk stalls.

To make the toys in this book you don't have to be a woodworking guru, nor do you have to be strong, gifted, or own a fortune in high-tec tools. All we ask is that you get involved with gusto, relish, zip and oomph! — the rest will all follow. What else can we say, except have fun!

# CONTENTS

*Yesterdays' children had all manner of wooden, folk made playthings: water toys with paddles, wind up toys with strings and pulleys, toys that rocked, whistled, walked, talked and played music, but best of all were the toys that moved.*

*A traditional carved and painted Mr Punch; Punch and Judy type puppet shows have always been popular with children and adults. A doll? A moving toy with pivotal limbs? An adult toy? certainly Mr Punch is all of these.*

## INTRODUCTION

'There is only one reason why all grown up people do not play with toys, and it is a fair reason. The reason is that playing with toys takes so very much more time and trouble than anything else.'

G. K. Chesterton

There was a time, a time before this, when if a child wanted a plaything, the parents or grandparents jolly well set-to with a hammer, wood and glue and made one. Not for yesterdays' children a plethora of plastics, and a maze of micro-chips — no, they had all manner of imaginative, beautifully made, wooden toys. Water toys with paddles and boilers, wind up toys with strings and pulleys, toys with wheels and whistles, wooden dolls that walked and talked, music box toys from Germany, curious carved toys from the Orient, toys to rock and ride, and so I could go on. Yes — as far as toys are concerned, yesterdays' children lived in a golden age. But best of all these wonderful wooden playthings were the folk made, moving toys.

It has been said that many experiments with basic physical principles of matter and energy were first realized in the form of simple-movement toys or toy automata. Balance and counterbalance, the wheel, the pendulum, flight, pulleys and cams; they all appeared as the motive force for toys, hundreds and even thousands of years before they were developed for adult use.

In this book we tell you about such delights as 'penny toys', 'folk toys', 'fairings' and 'country rustic playthings', and then we take you straight to the heart of the craft and show you how to make ten wonderfully exciting traditional moving toys.

*A Victorian Noah's Ark with animals, woodcarved and painted. On a Sunday in many strict religious households the children could only play with 'Sunday Toys'. A large wooden ark, and dozens of beautiful little animals scattered over the playroom floor – not a bad way to spend a Sunday?*

We know how difficult it can be to 'see' just how such and such a toy is put together, and we appreciate that many readers will be raw beginners, so with this in mind we have gone overboard with the 'how-to-do' illustrations. My wife Gill has watched me sawing and drilling, and I've analysed just how she manages her paints and brushes, and how she puts the toy together – then we've both sat down and carefully illustrated and described every step of the way. Maybe you don't know the difference between a pivotal rod and peach pip, and perhaps you've never considered working a craft at home – no matter, with our working drawings and 'hand-on-tool' illustrations, we gently guide you through all the designing and making stages. Each of our toy

*A Victorian pull-along toy; wooden carved and painted toys of this type and character have always been popular – what a beautiful imaginative toy.*

making projects has been considered in great detail; we tell you about the ethnic and folk origins, then we illustrate the designing, cutting, drilling, gluing, sanding, painting, putting together, and much much more. Wooden Toymaking is a stimulating inspirational craft, and home made toys are beautiful!

Well, enough of the praise and promise, roll up your sleeves, set out the wood, arrange the tools, and make a toy. Give our jaw snapping Crunchy Croc to a child, place our Hussar on a shelf, give our Meandering Man to your boss, and then sit back and watch the children and adults at play. Could it be that toys better express our desires and dreams than the real objects that they represent?

## TOYMAKERS DATA

TOOLS, TECHNIQUES, MATERIALS AND WORKSHOP

How many tools does a beginner need? Should we tell you in minute detail how best to use pencils and brushes? Should we take it that you the reader have some basic woodwork experience? It's all a bit of a problem! Well – we've just carried out our own mini survey, that is, talked to the postman, chatted to an old man who used to carve model aircraft toys; you know the sort of thing, World War II Heinkel raiders and Spitfires, questioned craft teachers, and also had long discussions with a young lad who started making wooden toys for a school project. And, would you believe? these parties all

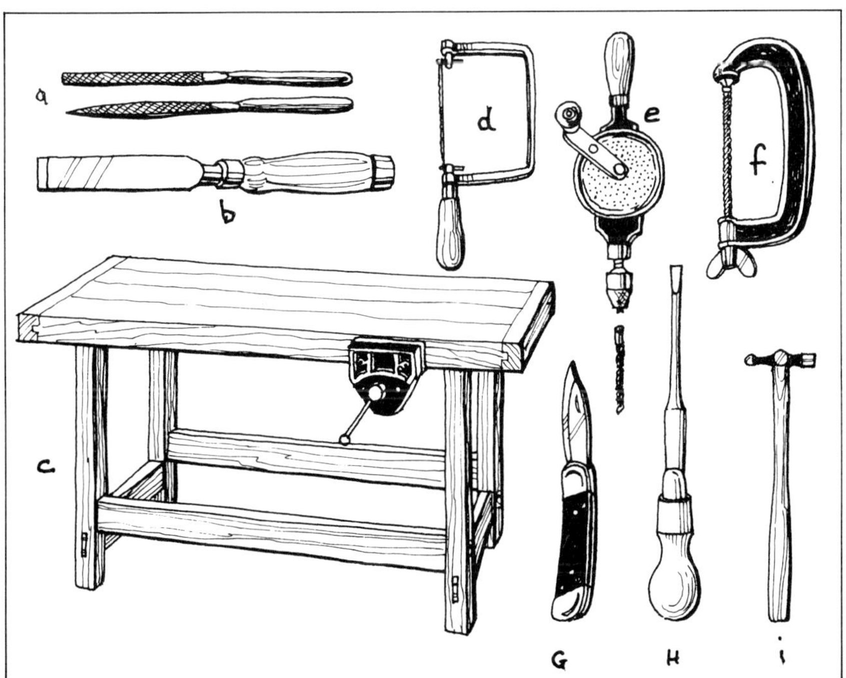


*(a) small model makers files. (b) a small chisel. (c) a stout workbench complete with vice. (d) a coping saw. (e) a small hand drill and bit. (f) a G-clamp. (g) a penknife (h) a screwdriver. (i) A ball pein hammer.*

*Painting – Before you start painting, work out some sort of drying frame –we use an old cake rack.*

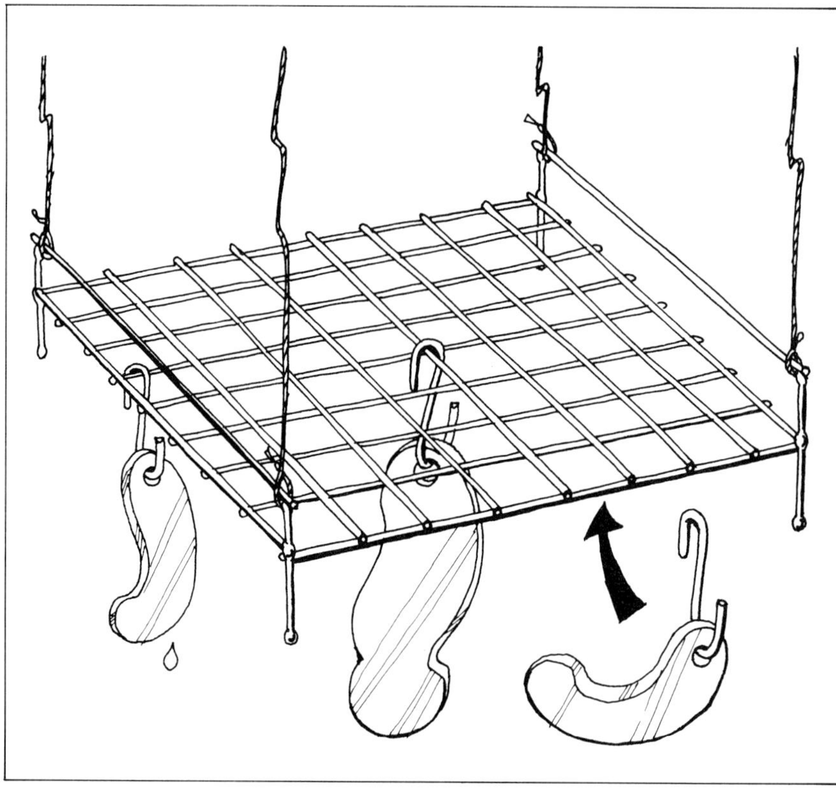

agree that, yes, yes, yes! definitions, descriptions and details on everything from 'Pivots' to 'Prototypes' are possibly a bit tedious, but never-the-less they are necessary.

How to cut a fine line with a coping saw, how to rub down wood prior to painting, how to organize your working area – these are all part and parcel of the craft of Wooden Toymaking, and as such they should just not be missed. Bench Clamps, Bobs, Bridle Joints, and Brushes . . . boring? unimportant? lightweight? . . . Not a bit of it – they're all beautiful!

**Beads** Okay so beads aren't essential to a toymakers needs, but my goodness they're useful. Glass beads for decorative details like 'eyes', large ceramic beads for bob-weights and pendulums, massive wooden beads for axle washers and counterbalances – I wouldn't be without them.

**Bench** A toymakers bench might be anything from a table in the kitchen, to a heavy trestle table in the garden, or even, come to that, a packing crate in the spare room. All that is required of a bench is that it be strong, stable, and solid enough to take clamps, hammer banging and sawing. Note – if you have to use the highly polished table in the dining room, use a cover-cloth or workboard, then you won't damage your tools!

**Bench Clamp/Vice** Meaning, a screw device for securing wood to the bench, or for pulling together two pieces of glued wood. There are any number of clamps, cramps and patent holdfasts on the market; if you are a beginner, start with a relatively inexpensive portable vice, then when you know your needs get something better.

**Bench Cloth** When you have cut, prepared and painted the component parts of a toy, then you need a bench cloth — that is to say, a piece of pattern-free sheeting, or such like, that can be spread over the bench. Such a cloth helps to focus attention, meaning that you won't lose small washers and pivot rods in a whole heap of bench scrap — it also keeps the newly painted parts clean and free from scratches.

**Blob-end Pins** If you are handy with an electric soldering iron, and you want to make small, delicate toys, then you might consider making pivot rods out of lengths of copper or brass wire that have been given soldered 'blob' or 'bead' ends.

**Bobs, or Bob-weights** Meaning a dangling weight or pendulum. A bob (see Chick project) might be made of clay, wood, brass or whatever — we like to use built-up bead bobs, because it is then possible to add or take away weight and so obtain a precise balance.

**Bridle Joint** Sometimes called an open mortise and tenon, bridle joints are frequently used as hinge joints — little flexible links between say a train and a carriage, doll and puppet limb joints and so on (see the Snake project).

**Brushes** These come in a great many shapes and sizes — we use large and small, soft, long haired, fine-point artists brushes. Brushes of this type improve with use, so buy the best, keep them clean, and always store them bristle up.

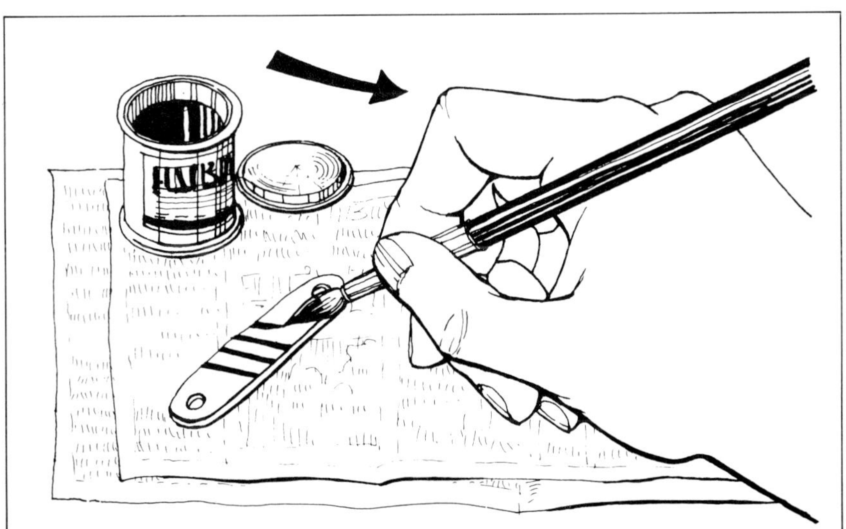

*Painting — Once you have given the toy components their ground colour, wait a while for the paint to dry, then take a fine-point brush and very carefully pick out the design details. Work with a clean dragging stroke, don't overload the brush and only use the tip.*

*The coping saw – note how in this instance the wood to be sawn is held firm with a G-clamp. Work with an even unhurried stroke, and try all the while to keep the blade at 90° to the working face of the wood.*

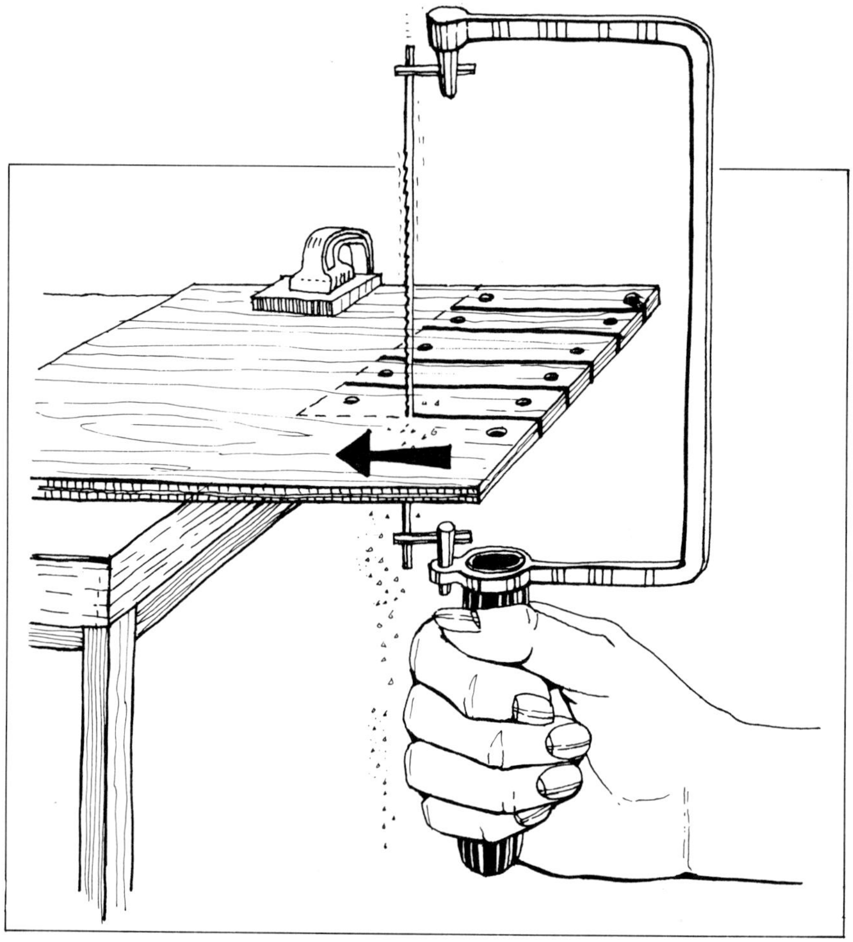

**Chisel** A flat-bladed, hand held tool – in use it can be held in one hand and then pushed with the other, or it can be held in one hand and banged with a mallet. Note – if you are a beginner, and you would rather not spend out on a large number of tools, then you can get away with using a good long-bladed pocket knife.

**Clamps** There are clamps, cramps, holdfasts, G-clamps and so on – we reckon that for starters, a beginner toymaker needs a vice to hold the wood while it is being sawn, and a G-clamp for holding glued wood.

**Compass** A two-leg instrument used to draw out circles and arcs. Yes, you can make-do with pins, pencils and bits of string, but as likely as not you'll find yourself going round in circles. Much better to buy a good quality long-leg compass – one that will securely hold a pencil.

**Coping Saw** A thin-bladed frame saw used for cutting a small section or sheet wood. The 'G' shaped frame has swivel spigots at each end, and these are designed to take fine flexible blades. Because the blades can be fitted, removed and refitted, all in a few moments, this type of saw is just perfect for working tight shapes and enclosed holes. Note – the blade can be fitted with the teeth pointing towards the handle, in which case you cut on the 'pull' stroke – or they can point away from the handle so that you cut on the 'push'.

Our advice is to try both ways of working, and then to go for the way that suits you.

**Copper Rod** Toymakers tend to use any amount of copper, brass and white metal rod for rivets, axles, counterbalances, springs and decorative detailing. We never reckon to pay out for wire rod but usually ask around, and then use salvaged heavy duty electrical wire, coat-hanger wire and such like.

**Counterbalance** Many small traditional simple-movement toys use a counterbalance for the motive force — meaning a weight or force that balances or offsets another (see the Hussar project).

**Crimp-end and Cap-end Rods** Meaning wires, rods and rivets. There are on the market any number of small, easy-to-use patent rods and pivotal fixings, some good and others not so good. However as we personally like 'all wood' toys, ones that are safe for toddlers, inexpensive, and easy to repair, we nearly always go for hardwood dowel pivotal rods. Note — if you do decide to use patent crimp-end type rivets or fixings, make sure that they are non-toxic, rust resistant and child-proof.

**Designing** Meaning to work out the structure or form of a toy by making a sketch, outline, pattern or working prototype. We usually start by visiting museums, galleries and old book shops, then sit back with a cup of tea and masses of workout paper. After working what we consider to be a good design, we then build a working model with bits of card, string and pins. Our

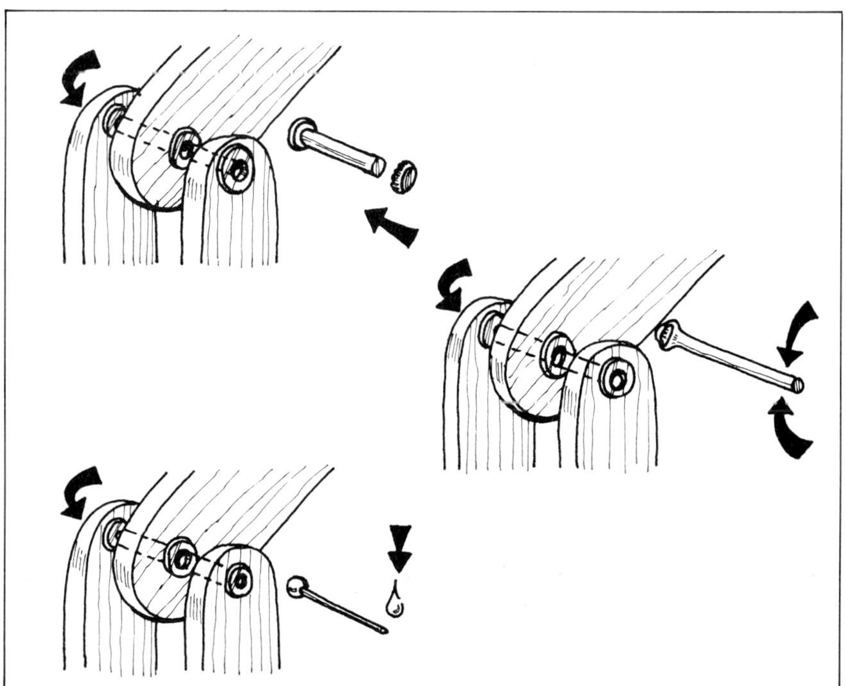

*Pivotal Fixings — (a) a patent crimp-end pivot rod — the rod is slid into position, then a small tool is used to fix the crimp cap. (b) squash end pivot rods can be made up from salvaged scrap wire — the pin is pushed home then the ends of the pin are spread with a hammer or punch. (c) Blob-end pins — the pin is slid home, washers are positioned, then the end of the pin is blobbed with a soldering iron.*

*When you are using a hand drill, support the wood to be drilled with a waster or backing board, and as with sawing, keep the drill at right angles to the wood. Don't rush or try to force the pace.*

advice is to always make a prototype — it saves spoiling wood. Finally, when the whole toy is worked out, we use gridded paper to draw it to size, and then finish up by drawing up a cutting list, a materials list and a costing.

**Designing Adjusting or Modifying** If you like the idea of such and such a toy, but want to make it smaller, larger, or whatever, then it is most important that you rework the design in total. For example — if your toy is to be 12 inches long, rather than the 6 inches, as described in our working drawings, then you must ask yourself — should the wood be thicker? Do the pivot rods need to be stronger? Is the larger toy child proof and hazard-free? Does the simple-movement part of the toy still work? These are all points that need careful consideration.

**Dowel, Hardwood Rod, or Dowel Pegs** Dowel, meaning a smooth, machine turned, hardwood rod, is without doubt a prime toymaking material. In its many sizes, everything from a fat 1½ inches diameter, 'bannister' dowel, down to a slender $^{3}/_{16}$ inch hard, close-grained, birch dowel, it has thousands of uses. It can be made into axle rods, it can be sliced into wheels, it can be tapered for masts, carved for doll limbs, and so on. A traditional material of this character is strong, easy to use, and inexpensive.

**Drilling Holes and Hand Drills** Many woodworkers advocate the use of power drills, because they take large and small bit sizes, and they can drill at great speed — very nice too, but is this what a toymaker requires? Well we for one think not. Take our advice, get yourself a beautifully simple, inexpensive, silent running, easy to use, totally controllable, hand operated drill, and it will last a life-time. When you want to drill a hole, select the right size drill bit for the job, support the wood to be drilled with a waster or

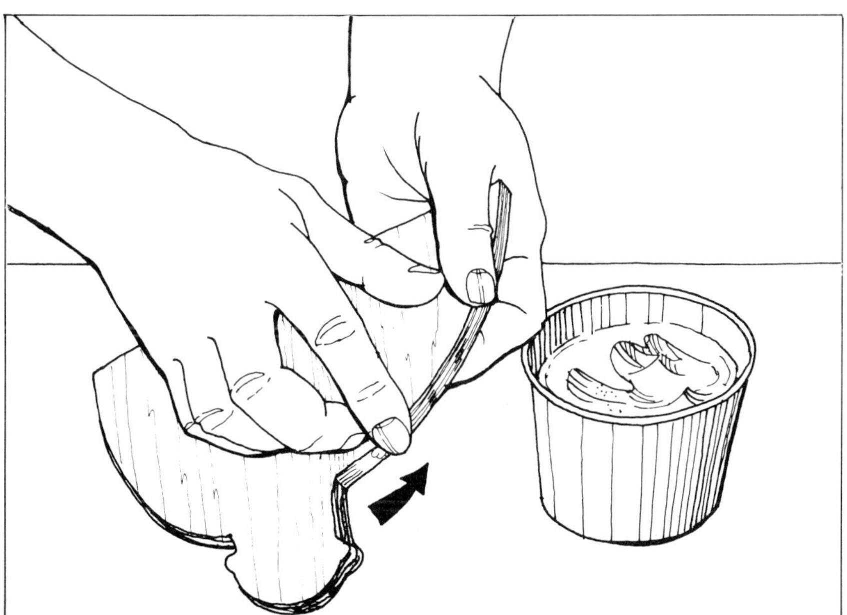

*Filling — as likely as not, there will be small cavities at the edges of the sawn ply; fill these before rubbing down.*

backing board, and then secure the whole works in a clamp or vice. Now, take your time, no hurry; position the drill, line it up so that it is going to enter the wood at the correct angle and finally hold it steady with one hand, and set it in motion with the other.

**Felt Tip Pens** Meaning the ordinary inexpensive felt nibbed pens — they are brightly coloured and come in large packs. It is inadvisable to use pens of this character for fine presentation work, but they are certainly very useful when it comes to making quick museum sketches, or for knocking up instant, 'how it could look', visuals.

**Files and Shaping Rasps** Every toymaker needs a selection of files and rasps, say a model makers 'needle' file for working rivet heads and metal axle rods, riffler files for cutting sculptural shapes and tight curves, and maybe one of the Surform type rasps for working multiply edges and curves.

**Fillers** What to say about fillers? Well, we always use a car body type resin/hardener filler, because it is permanent and easy to use, it cuts and saws like wood, and it doesn't break down even after being soaked day in and day out with toddler saliva. Mix a little filler at a time, as directed by the manufacturer, let it dry, and then work it as for wood.

**Fret Saw** Fifty or sixty years ago, fretwork hobbies swept the land, and Schoolboy Annuals of the period described how to make such little gems as trains, ships, glove boxes, collar boxes, book-ends and radio speaker boxes — Ah! it's all coming back (well not really). Fret saws are akin to coping saws, in that they have a flexible easily removed blade, and a 'G' frame; their 20 inch frames make it possible to cut well into a large sheet of ply, but then again their fragile blades are only really suitable for thin plys. Note — if you are a beginner, go for the coping saw.

**Glues and Adhesives** There are animal skin and bone glues that have to be heated up, there are electric hot glue guns, there are rubber glues in tubes, contact adhesives in cans, and so on. There are hundreds of products to choose from; it's a tricky sticky area, but we reckon that for toymaking you can't beat a polyvinyl acetate glue, or PVA for short. A glue of this type is usually packaged in plastic squeezy nozzle bottles, there is no waste, it's not messy or smelly, and it's got a long life. In fact PVA is perfect for most small home based wood crafts. To use, it is smeared over one or the other of the surfaces that are to be stuck, then the pieces of wood are brought together and either weighted or clamped. Finally, the glue ooze is wiped off with a damp cloth, and then the whole works is left for twenty-four hours to dry and cure. Note — in its wet state, PVA glue is water soluble, so spills and splobs can be wiped up with a wet cloth.

**Grids** Meaning scaled grids that are placed over working drawings. You can buy grid paper, or you can draw up your own. It's all very straightforward; you decide just how large, or how small, you want your toy to be, then you copy and rework our designs a square at a time. So for example if you choose a project that has a scale of say one little square to 1 inch, all you do is to take a piece of full size 1 inch grid paper, and transfer our design lines square-by-square. Once you have scaled up the design or pattern in this way, you can trace it direct, and finally transfer the traced shapes to your wood.

**Hammer** Hammers come in all shapes and sizes — everything from a 'De Lux Joiners' hammer, through to 'peins', 'balls', 'claws' and 'magnetic'. If you are a hammerless beginner, take a trip to an ironmongers, and get yourself a good quality '4 oz, ash handled, Ball Pein' — the perfect hammer for toymaking.

**Inspirational Material** Any toymaker worth his/her salt is going to be on the lookout for fresh ideas. Magazine clips, photographs showing early twentieth century European folk crafts, museum catalogues and old books — these might all be described as inspirational. In the last month or so, we have found a photograph of an old Polish toy in a 1950 Geographical Magazine, we have visited two folk/craft museums, and we spotted a modern folk toy in a charity shop. Toymaking is not just a craft, it's a way of life.

**Iron Block** Meaning a small anvil — we use an old flat iron that we put, handle-down, in the vice — it's just perfect for riveting, wire bending, nail squashing, and all those other little jobs that can't be worked on the new tile worksurface or the best room table.

**Knife** Toymakers tend to use and adopt just about any knife that does the job in hand, for example, we use an old kitchen knife, a large Victorian bread knife, a beautiful bone handled penknife and a modern chip carving knife. Note — we favour old knives — ones that have stained blades; they're stronger, and they seem to stay sharper longer.

**Laminating** In the context of this book, laminating means to take several sheets of ply and to glue them together sandwich-like. So, for example, you might use four thicknesses of ¼ inch multiply to make a laminated component that is 1 inch thick. Working in this way not only makes for easier tooling, but it is also an economical way of making a toy from a single sheet of wood.

**Metal Rod** Meaning lengths of round section wire that can be used for axles, pivots, rivets and such like. These can usually be begged or borrowed, or if the worse come to the worse bought from a hobby shop or ironmongers. Best if you use copper or brass, but if funds are tight, use aluminium or even salvaged coat-hanger wire.

**Mortise and Tenon** A woodworkers joint — mortise being a hole, slot or recess that is worked and shaped to take a matching projection, or tenon (see the Chick project). Our advice to 'never done it before' raw beginners is to cut the mortise small and the tenon large, and then to slowly nibble and scrape away with a file and sandpaper until they are a good fit. Okay, so it's not beautiful woodwork, but it gets you there in the end.

**Multiply** Toys need to be child-proof, free from dangerous splinters, and most important of all, they need to be strong. Yes you can certainly use traditional woods like beech, sycamore, mahogany or even oak, but these do have their problems. For example, oak has a tendency to split, beech can be twisted, grainy and very difficult to work, and, of course, all natural 'plank' woods are likely to split on short-grain areas. Well, not so with multiply sheet wood; it's very strong, it's beautiful to work and it can be purchased in thicknesses from $^1/_8$ inch, $^3/_{16}$ inch, $^1/_4$ inch, right up to 1 inch. Now when we say use such and such a thickness of ply or multiply, we don't mean that you should use that coarse centred, impossible to work sheet wood that goes by such names as, 'block ply', 'stout heart' or 'Malaysian'; it's difficult to cut, it's soft, and it's altogether horrible. No!, when we say use ply or multiply, we are referring to the type of laminated ply that is built up in thin $^1/_{16}$ inch veneer layers. A plywood of this character has a smooth, white, close-grained face, it's tremendously strong, it can be intricately worked without the danger of it breaking across slender 'necks' and it can be worked and sanded so that all faces and edges are smooth. If you are a raw beginner, be on your guard when you are buying wood, ask for multiply, and don't be fobbed off with anything else. Note – a sheet of $^1/_4$ inch thick multiply should be made up of four or five thin veneer layers.

**Nails** If possible, don't use them; they rust, and they're not a good idea for 'toddler sucking' toys. If you have to use them, go for brass pins, but better still, use glue, screws, rivets, or nuts and bolts.

**Paints and Painting** When you come to painting, always wipe down your dusty worksurface with a damp cloth, and carefully set out your brushes and materials. Now as you probably know, some paints and finishes contain lead and other toxic materials, so you do have to be wary. With these problems in mind we asked around and were assured that all modern paints, or, at least

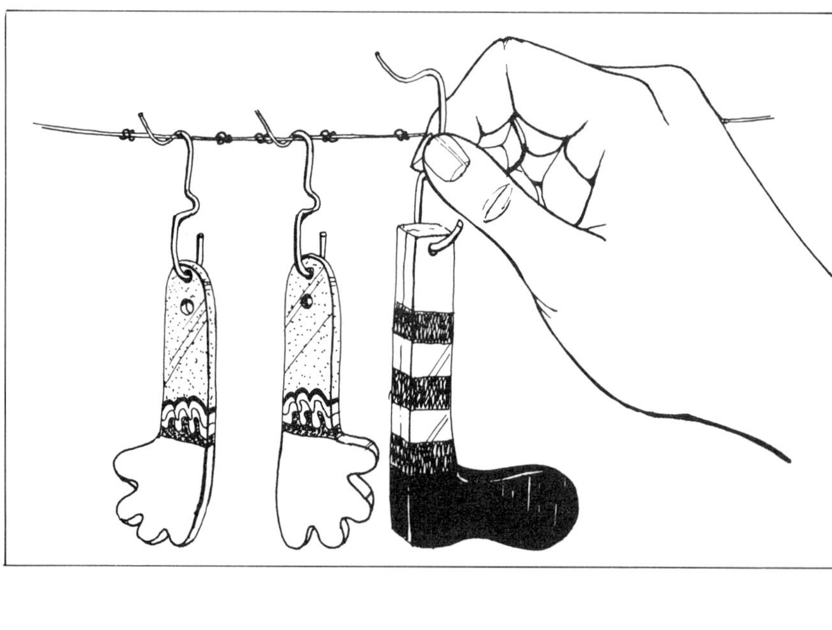

*Painting – painted components can be hung from a line – we make hanging hooks out of paper clips, and knot the line so that the pieces can't slide along and touch each other.*

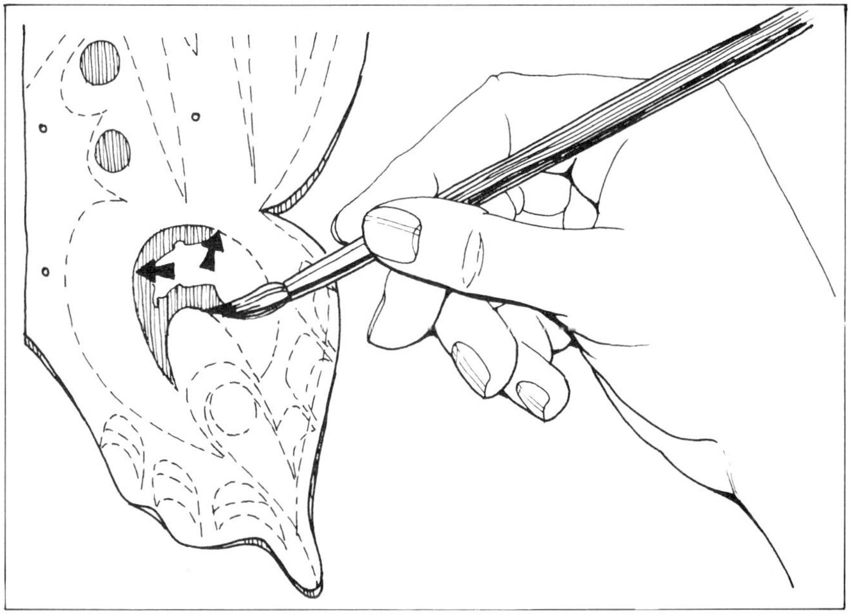

*Painting – when you have established just how you want the designs and motifs to be, take a fine-point brush and some well mixed paint, and very carefully line-in the design. See how the fine-pointed brush hairs drag and sweep round the inside of the motif to be painted.*

those used commercially for painting toys and other child related goods, are required by law to meet certain non-toxic lead-free standards. Now for the tricky bit – when we made first hand contact with a well known paint manufacturer, they said that although their paints certainly came within safety standards, they didn't necessarily come up to the standards as required by the 'Toy Safety Act' – see what we mean about tricky? Anyway, the

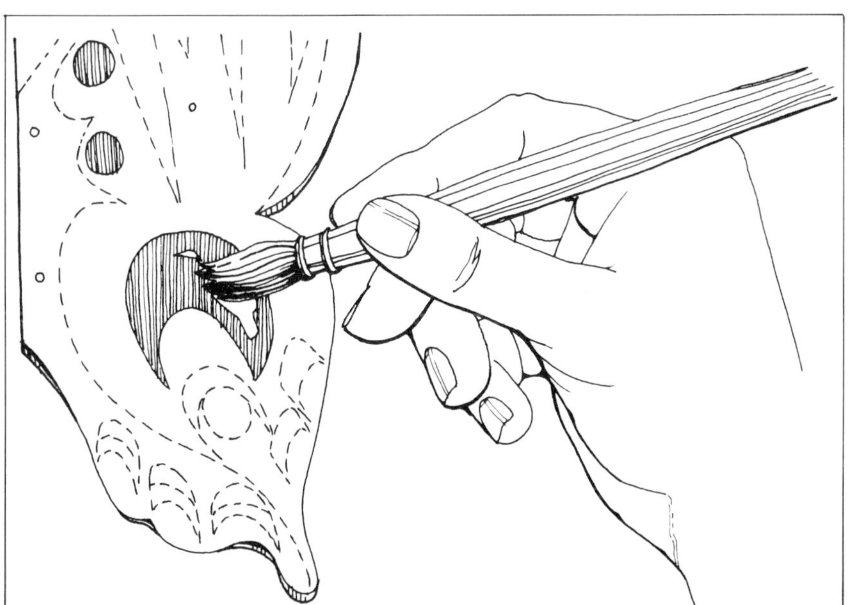

*Painting – Once you have lined-in the motif to be painted, use a larger brush to block in the colour.*

considered advice is to play it safe and only to use Humbrol or Air-Fix model makers paints — they come in small tins, they're fast drying and brilliantly coloured, and most important of all, they are designed with children in mind. Note — while you are buying your top coat gloss paints, you might as well get yourself a recommended primer (white), and an undercoat.

So now your area is organized and all your tools and materials are to hand. First lay on a white primer, making sure you work it well into edges, grain and holes, then you let it dry before you rub it down with a fine grade of sandpaper. Next you lay on an undercoat, then you let this dry before you rub it down with sandpaper. Now you clean out all pivotal holes, making sure that there are no wet blobs, then you lay on a thin gloss top coat. Finally, take a fine-point brush and a selection of well mixed colours, and pick out all the patterns, designs and details.

Of course there are any number of possible problem areas; the wood to be painted must be well prepared, no dust, splinters or greasy finger marks; you mustn't mix paints of a different brand or type, say a car paint on top of a household paint; you shouldn't paint in a wet damp atmosphere and so we could continue — muttering on about paint fumes, toxic brush cleaners, the dangers of smoking or eating while you are painting and so on. However, if you have any doubts at all as regards materials or techniques, take a piece of scrap wood through all the painting stages.

**Pencils** You might ask, what is there to say about pencils? and the answer would be, quite a lot! For example, we always use a good quality soft 2B for designing and tracing, then line-in the back of the tracing with a 3B, and

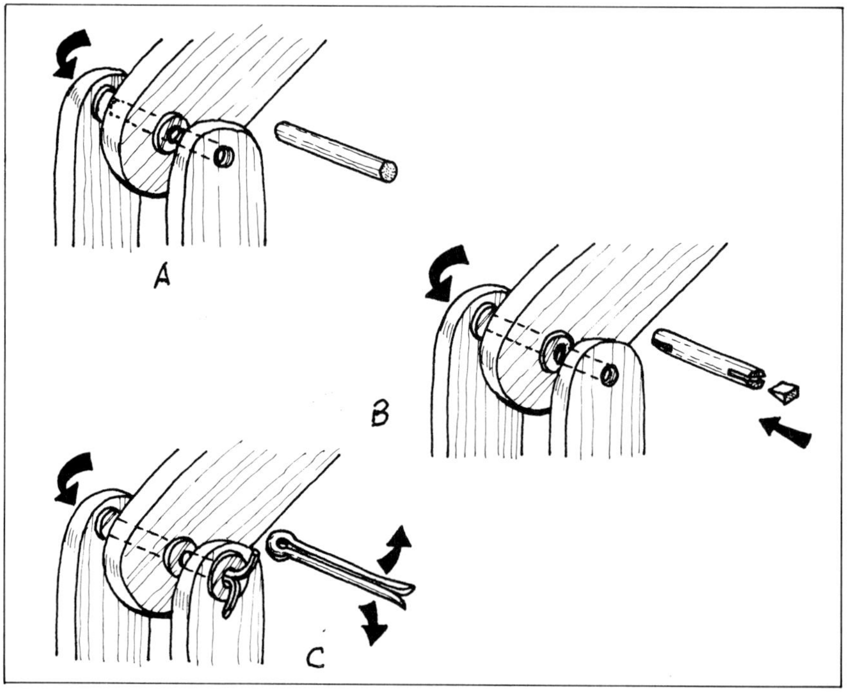


*Pivotal fixings — (a) a glue-end dowel and washers. (b) a wedge and glue dowel and washers. (c) cotter pin and washers. Consider the toy, decide how strong or not so strong the pivotal pins need to be, then choose your fixing accordingly.*

finally do the pencil-press transferring with an 'H'. And of course when the designs have been transferred to the wood, we line-in and label the drawn shapes with a soft pencil. Don't think that this chopping and changing around with pencil types is a faddy idiosyncrasy, no, we learned, over the years, that these particular pencils, used in this way, make for a first class job. Note — never ever line-in and label the wood with hard pencils or felt tip markers — hard pencils leave incised lines and some felt tip pens have a nasty habit of bleeding through the paint.

**Pendulum** Meaning a weight or bob, hung on a thread or cord, so that it can swing freely under the influence of gravity. In toymaking, pendulum bobs can be made out of just about anything wood, glass beads, ceramic beads, lead or even some 'found' item like say the brass bob from a builders plumb line (see Chick project). Note — with a pendulum, the shorter the thread the faster the swing, and vice versa.

**Pivotal Points and Rods** In the context of this book, a pivotal rod, a pivot point, or even just a pivot are all short shafts on which a component turns or swings, e.g. wheel/axle and limb joint.

**Profiles** The initial ply cut-outs or blanks might be termed profiles — when we say . . . work such and such a profile to a good smooth, round finish, we mean take a knife, file and sandpaper, and work the wood until all the sawn edges and corners are completely smooth to the touch and so ready to be painted.

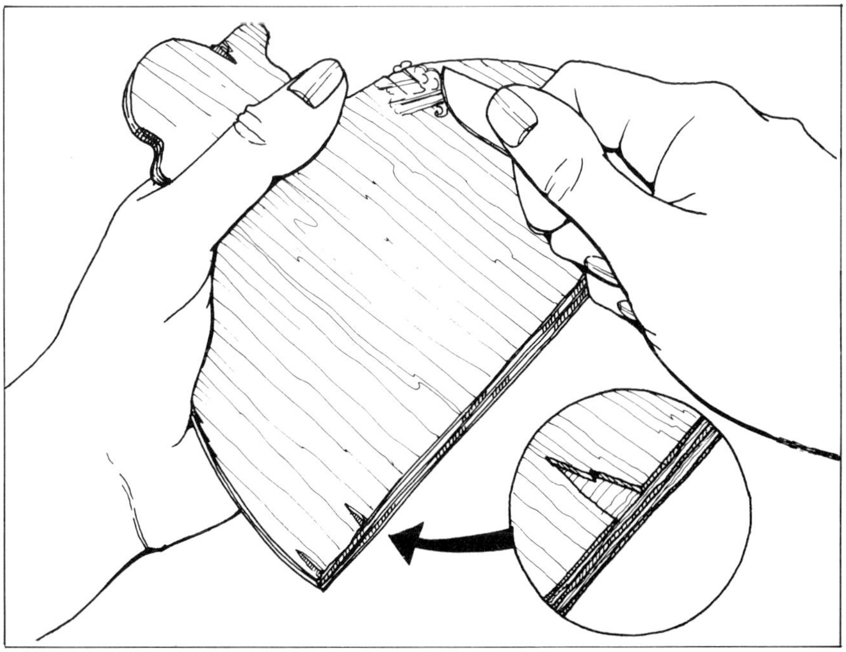

*Filling — mix a small amount of resin/hardener filler, work it into all the grain splits and tears, leave it proud and let it dry.*

**Prototype** Meaning the initial working model upon which the final design is based. So, if you want to rework or modify one of our designs, or you aren't quite sure how our toy/toys move, fit together or work, then you will need to knock up a working model or prototype. For example when we designed the Croc, we couldn't see how the jaw movement related to the turn of the cams, so we made a working model with scraps of card, staples, bits of string and sticky tape.

**PVA Glue** Meaning Polyvinyl Acetate (P.V.A.) (see Glue).

**Resin Filler** Wood splints, torn grain, ragged holes and cavities in sawn edges — these all need to be filled and sanded prior to painting. Don't use putty or plaster, as recommended in old books, because they both tend to dry and crack, but rather use a two part resin/hardener filler of the type used to patch car bodies.

All you do is to mix a small amount of resin to hardener, as directed, then smear it in the tear or hole so that it's proud, leave it for a short while to harden, then finally you rub it down and paint as for wood.

**Rubbing Down** Meaning to take a rough-sawn ply blank, and to work it to a smooth, ready-to-paint finish. We usually cut off the corners and burrs with a knife, have a swift rub over with a coarse sandpaper, go over the piece with a filler, and finally work through the coarse-to-smooth graded sandpapers.

Note — rubbing down is messy, so best if you can work in the great outdoors, then you won't clog up your breathing tubes with potentially harmful wood dust.

**Sanding and Sandpapers** Sandpapers or glasspapers are best purchased in a graded pack; meaning a pack that contains a range of degrees of coarseness. In such a pack, you might have a sheet of 'Strong 2' which is the coarsest, a sheet of 'O', which is the finest, and then a selection of grades in between.

In use, you need to wrap the sandpaper round a support, and this might be anything from your thumb to a clothes-peg, then you just rub away until the wood is 'toddler-sucking' smooth. Note — if you dampen the wood slightly to raise the grain, let it dry, and then rub off the raised grain hairs; you will achieve a super-fine finish. We usually use the sandpapers in the order of coarseness — 'M2', 'F2' and then '1'.

**Saws and Sawing** Throughout, we mention any number of saw types: fret saws, band saws, bow saws and so on, and of course they do all have their uses.

However, for making small wooden toys, we reckon that you can't beat a good quality coping saw. Now a saw of this character is flexible, in all senses of the word — it's simple to use, it's inexpensive, but best of all, the blade can quickly be removed. The blade can be unclipped, passed through a previously drilled hole, and refitted, all in a few moments, thus enabling you to swiftly cut out an enclosed curve or hole — a very useful tool.

**Scissors** Every toymaker needs a pair of scissors, or better still two pairs. We use three pairs, a massive pair for hacking out heavy card prototypes, a cheap pair of wallpaper scissors for cutting bits of this and that, everything from wire to tin cans and a little pair of nail scissors for fiddly trimmings and finishing.

**Simple-movement Toys** Meaning that the movement of the toys relates to some basic, traditional, easy to understand motive force. No batteries, no mind cramming electro-magnetic micro-chip horrors or such like – just straightforward levers, pendulums and counterbalances . . . beautiful!

**Stick-Tools** Over the years we have made a collection of stick-tools, meaning various pieces of shaped wood that we use to support the sandpaper when we are rubbing down. For example, we have a couple of old dolly pegs, an old ruler, half a dozen bits of scrap dowel, a piece of 2×1 inch, a bit of triangular section wood, and so on. You can't buy a stick-tools, you'll be glad to know – they can only be 'found', made or gathered. Note – next time you go to the sea-side, an hour or two spent beach combing should set you up with a good stick-tool collection.

**Split Pins or Cotter Pins** Cotter pins, made of brass of course, and used with washers, are a very simple means of fastening together two sheets of ply, say for the limbs of the clown. However, a strong nimble fingered youngster might be able to undo such a fixing, and the bent-back bit of the pin can be sharp and scratchy, so use with care.

**Squash-end Pins** Meaning brass, copper or alumina pivotal rods. The wire rod is cut to size and slid into place, the washers are positioned, then the ends of the rod are slightly squashed or flattened with say pliers or a hammer. A fixing of this type is swift, inexpensive, efficient and permanent.

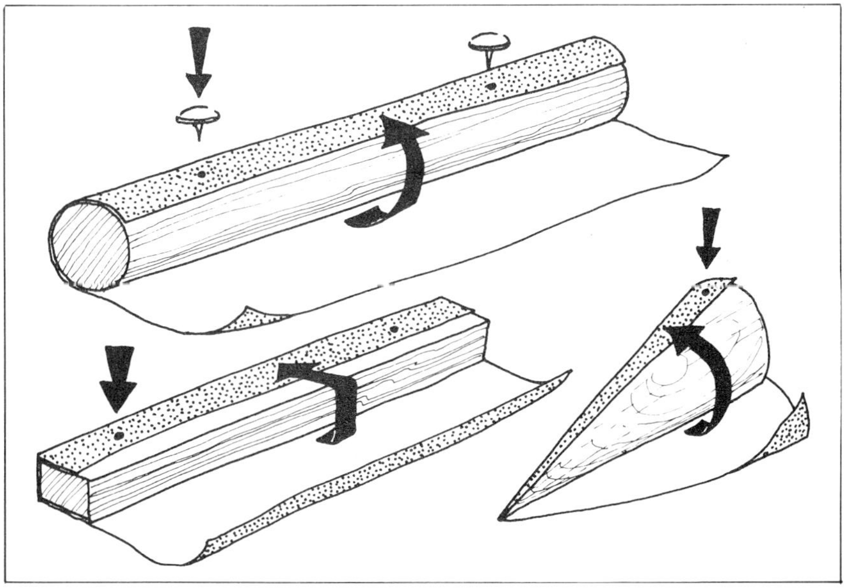

*Stick-tools – stick-tools can be used to support the sandpaper when you are rubbing down profiles; we have a 'found' collection of tools, pegs, dowel, 2×1 inch lolly sticks – they can all be used.*

**Tracing Paper** We always use a good quality tracing paper of the grade 'smooth' and the weight '112'. We work up a master drawing, trace the drawing, line-in the reverse side of the tracing and finally we use a hard pencil to press transfer the traced lines onto the working surface of the wood.

Yes, we've tried all manner of cheap flimsy tracing papers, everything from bakers tissue to poorer grades of wrapping tissue, but by the time we've traced, lined-in and pencil pressed, these papers are a half useless mess of tatters. We reckon that the best quality papers are the cheapest in the long run.

**Undercoat** For a top class finish, the wood certainly needs to be well primed and given at least one undercoat, but if you want to achieve a finish that is the best of the best, then you might need to lay on two or even three undercoats (see projects and 'Painting').

**Washers** Made of brass or wood, washers should always be used between moving parts. We use wooden washers for distance pieces and spacers, and brass when we reckon to have rivets, cotter pins, squash-ends or nuts and bolts.

**Wasters or Backing Boards** When you are drilling, or even sawing a piece of ply, it's a good idea to use a piece of scrap wood behind the wood that's being worked, then the tools will be less likely to burst through the ply in one great, grain ripping, rush.

**Working Drawings** Meaning well worked and scaled drawings — not scribbles on the back of old scraps of paper, but rather carefully considered drawings that show wood size, toy size, sections, details, moving parts, colours, materials list and so on. And when you've got your master drawing, never cut it up and use it for a pattern — always take a tracing.

**Working Face** Meaning either the side of the wood on which you have drawn the shapes, or the side of the wood that is most on view when the toy has been made up.

**Workout Paper** When you are working out the initial toy designs, you'll need as much cheap scrap paper as you can get hold of. We visit a local printers and ask for off-cuts, and usually they give us enough for all our needs. If you have choice, ask for white, slightly matt, cartridge type paper.

**Workshop** In the context of this book, a toymaking workshop might be anything from a space in the kitchen, to a spare room, attic, garden shed, the garage, or even the one night a week use of a school evening class room. If it keeps the weather out, and it's got a bench come table, additional worksurfaces, a chair, a shelf or two and electricity, then we reckon that it can be called a workshop. As to the ideal working area — well that's something again, and not so easy to define, especially bearing in mind that our own workshop is no more than a cold, damp, badly lit Nissen hut complete with draughts, mice and spiders.

We would say that you need a compact, warmish, well lit area of about 100 square feet, so a space like a garage or a spare room would be just fine. Into this little haven, you have to cram as many worksurfaces and storage spaces as possible. So for starters, and perhaps most important of all, you need one good solid workbench, complete with a vice or holdfast. This bench is your base or focal point, the place where you do most of your sawing, drilling, and hammering.

Now for the tricky bit; when you have cut and drilled the wood, it has to be rubbed down prior to painting, and this is where you have to start making compromises. Sanding and rubbing down produces wood dust, and you can take it from us, wood dust and painting just don't mix. So what to do? Well, you could do all the sanding outside in the garden, or you could do all the painting outside the workshop, in say the kitchen or whatever, or, then again, you could settle for a messy workshop, and only wipe down the corner that you have reserved for painting. As you can see, it needs a bit of thinking about. Okay, so you now have a central workbench, and areas set aside for preparation and painting.

Your next problem is the need for wall space and storage — you must have nails, hooks and pegs for tools — shelves, boxes and cupboards for toys that are in various stages of completion — shelves for paints — tins and jars for screws, washers and bolts — boxes for scrap wood — corners for new wood — pinboard for inspirational material — and so on and on. Ah! the smell of new wood, and the pleasure of seeing the toys take shape . . . mmm wonderful!

Finally, a workshop, be it ever so humble, is more than just an area set aside for manual work — it is a retreat where you can do your own thing. This is not to say of course that you can't have a radio or have a little corner set aside for a sit down and a cup of tea. If you start getting visits from friends, neighbours and 'finger nosey' children, then you can reckon that your toymaking workshop is all that it should be. Note — yes, woodshavings, sawdust and all the rest are certainly good fun, but they can also be a hazard; so sweep up regularly, check the electrics, and get yourself a fire extinguisher.

PROJECT ONE

# THE MEANDERING MAN

TOY TYPE · A DOLL WITH PIVOTAL-WHEEL LEGS

## THOUGHTS ON THE PROJECT

A doll to kiss, a doll to cry over, a doll to talk to — at some time or other, most of us have sought the bedtime clinging, cosy crying comfort of a doll. If you could go back to the dim and distant origins of man, and search around in the deepest darkest corners of the oldest and most primitive cave dwelling, almost certainly you would find a little model figure or doll. Okay, so some of the oldest dolls are little more than crudely shaped pieces of stone, bone or wood, but never-the-less dolls they are. Of course many tribal and folk dolls were conceived not as childish playthings, but more as fetishes and effigies; but even so, just like dolls, they still functioned as 'dark night' burden sharers. For example, the ancient Egyptians buried dolls with the dead; in medieval Europe fertility dolls were placed in the beds of childless couples; 'guardian' dolls were built into the fabric of English Elizabethan houses; African dolls were designed to be disease receiving scapegoats, and so we could go on.

Apparently a doll's life was sometimes a pretty grim business. Well not so with the 'Meandering Man' doll; he and his kind have probably spent the last hundred years or so happily walking through the nurseries and playrooms of Europe. As to his origins — Russian? Swiss? Polish? German? Swedish? — who can say! Certainly he looks a little like some of the early nineteenth century French cardboard cut-out Jumping Jack 'pantins', and then again like some of the American Colonial folk-rustic and whittled movable-limb dolls. No matter! — we have designed our modern Meandering Man to take the harshest, 'toddler sucking, wall bashing' treatment; he's a wonderfully smooth mover, a perfect pre-school action toy.

## CONSIDERING THE PROJECT

The Meandering Man is a beautiful toy, a real delight for children and adults alike; he's strong; he's easy to make; his nicely rounded form is just right for young, grasping, 'learning' hands, but best of all his wheel-turning walk is exciting and in the best 'action toy' traditions.

All that apart, with this project, it's a good idea at the onset to visit a toy museum, make notes and sketches, and then to sit back and consider possible design modifications. Make design sketches, work cardboard and sticky tape prototypes, and see if you can come up with a unique personalized toy.

This done, have a look at our working drawings and details and see how we have two design grids, one at four squares to one inch, and the other at two squares to one inch, a finished doll that is about five inches high and five inches wide, a total wood thickness of an inch, and note also how we have used ¼ inch multiply throughout. There is no getting away from the fact that the six-legged circle is a little bit tricky, because it involves the use of geometry. But that apart, the designing, cutting and putting together is straightforward and uncomplicated. Note — if you are a beginner, don't panic, we have explained every step of the way.

As for materials, we have chosen to stay with an 'all wood' toy, and have used hardwood dowel for the wheel pivot; but that is not to say that you can't use clip-fix metal pins, brass nuts and bolts, or even 'squash-end' rods — adjust the design to suit your own needs.

*Working Drawing, painting grid – note the scale of four squares to one inch. When you come to do the painting, don't fiddle and fuss around, go for a big bold 'cartoon' type design.*

## MATERIALS

For this project you need a piece of white faced ¼ inch multiply that measures about 16 × 14 inches, about 1¼ inch of ¼ inch diameter hardwood dowel, a quantity of white PVA glue and a selection of model makers paints, primer, undercoat and topcoat.

**Tools** As for tools, you need the use of a bench clamp or holdfast, a coping saw with some spare blades, a hand drill with a ¼ inch drill bit, a selection of

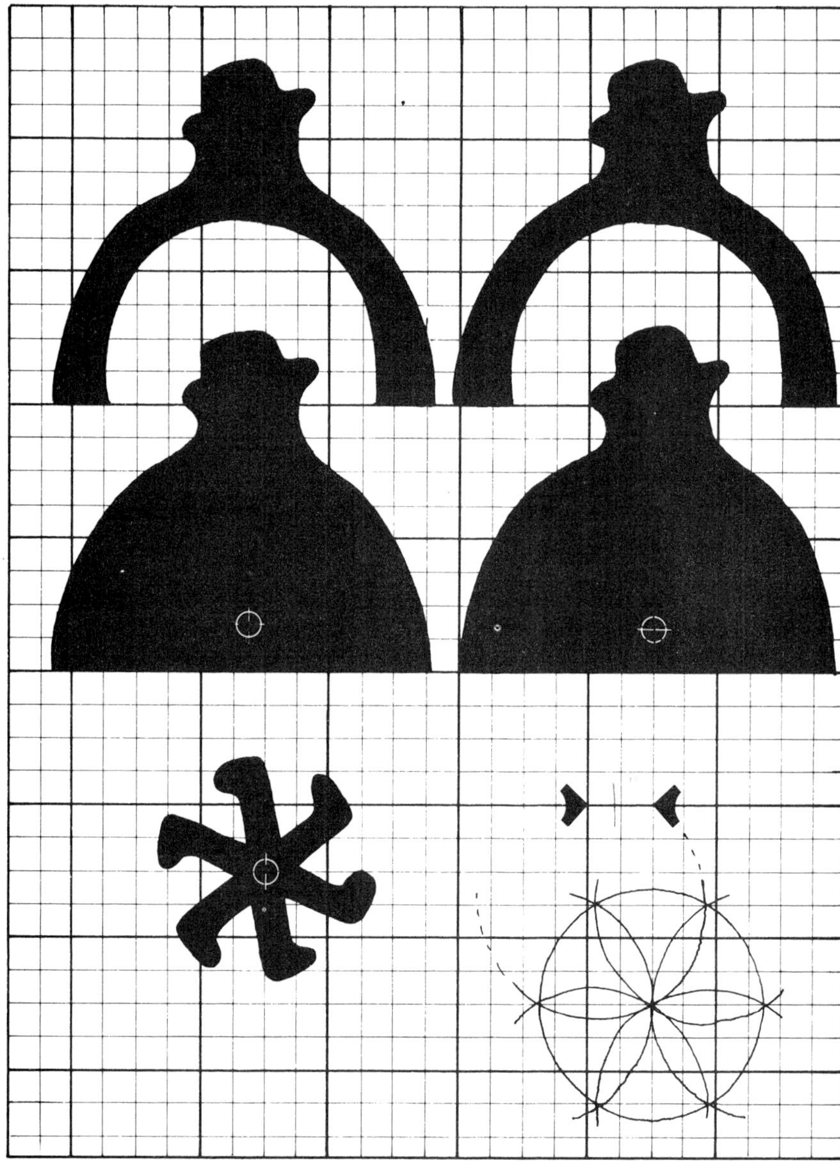

*Working Drawing, cutting grid – note the scale of two squares to one inch. There should be two side plates, two fillers or spacers and a single six-legged wheel. See also how the circle is subdivided into six equal parts.*

stick-tools, a pack of graded sandpapers, a small sharp knife, a metal ruler, a pair of compasses, a couple of good quality, long haired, fine point brushes and, of course, you're going to need all those 'around the house' bits and pieces like pencils, scrap paper, tracing paper, felt tip pens, paint tubs, cloths and cleaners.

## SETTING OUT THE DESIGN

Take your workout paper, compass and ruler — fix the compass at 1¾ inches,

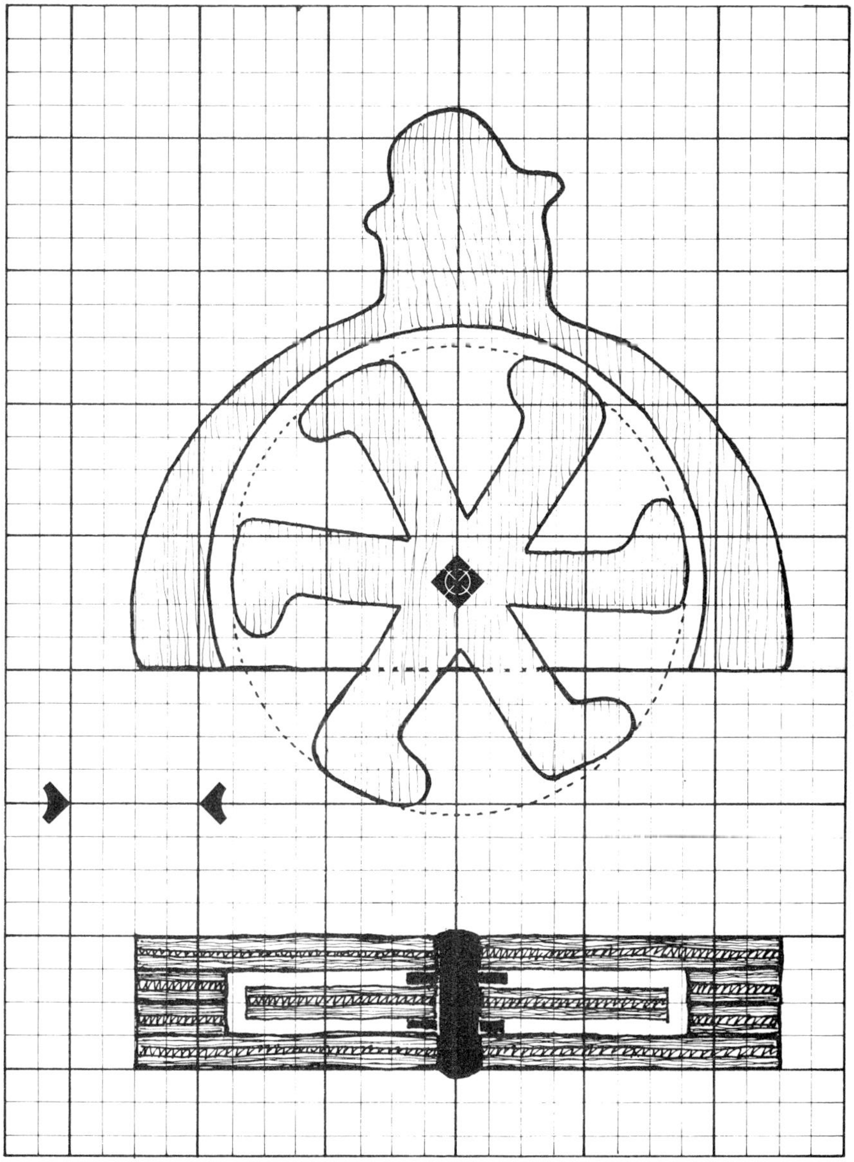

*Working Drawing, assembly grid – note the scale of four squares to one inch. See how the wheel is a snug fit within the body cavity, and how washers are slid on the dowel.*

then set out half a dozen or so circles. Now, with the compass still fixed at 1¾ inches, go round the circles striking off arcs — that is to say, six arcs with each circle. If all is correct, each of the six circles will now be nicely divided into six equal parts. This done, take a pencil and ruler, and go from circle to circle, drawing lines from the centres to the circumference arcs. Now take a scrap of tracing paper, select a circle, and then, using the six radius lines as guides, set about drawing the six-legged/footed wheel.

We've allowed the half a dozen circles, because there's bound to be a bit of trial, error and rubbing out. However, work from circle to circle, tracing and

*Use scrap paper and a compass to work out the six-legged wheel. Set the compass at a radius of 1¾ inches, draw a circle, then strike off arcs round the circumference – there should be six arcs for each circle.*

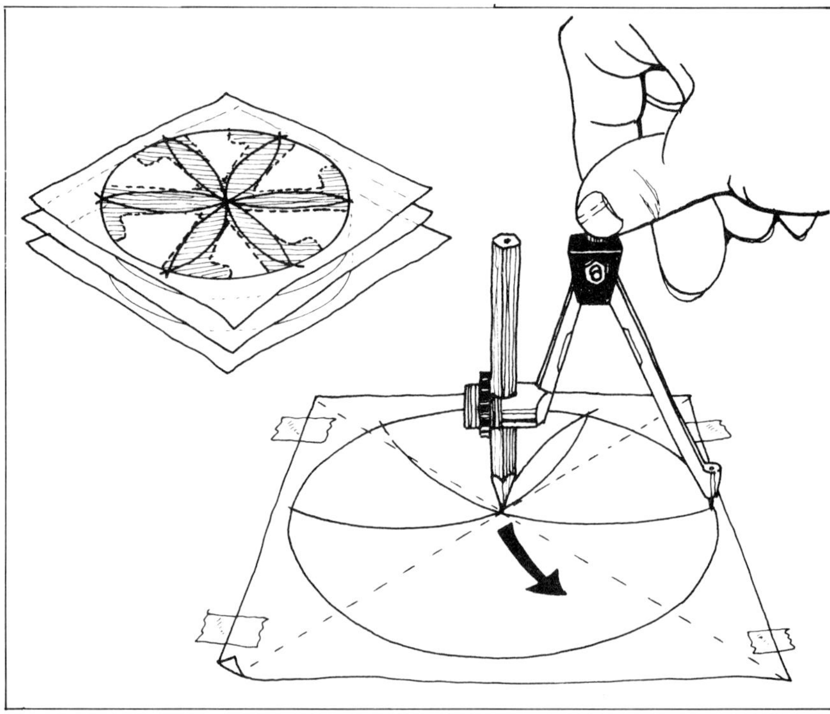

transferring, until you have achieved a single, well set out wheel. Now using this master wheel as your main reference, take your workout paper and draw out the Meandering Man's side panels and profile.

Finally, when you have a good looking design that works, take your tracing paper and pencil press transfer the lines of the design through to the working face of the multiply.

## CUTTING, GLUING AND DRILLING

When you have transferred the drawn shapes to the ply, stop a moment and check that all is correct. There should be five shapes in all – two side plates, two side plate distance pieces or spacers and a single six-legged wheel. It might be as well, at this stage, to label the shapes, and establish their working faces or 'best' sides. Now, take up the coping saw, put the wood in the vice, then start to carefully fret round the drawn shapes. Be mindful that the line of cut needs to be worked on the outside of the drawn line. And so you continue, manoeuvering the wood and the saw, until you have cut out all five shapes.

This done, take a couple of stick tools and sandpaper and clean up the inside curves of the two spacers, and the whole of the wheel. Don't worry too much about the spacers because they will, after all, be built into the toy; just make sure that they are free from sharp edges, corners and burrs. The wheel, however, needs to be well worked and rubbed down – aim for a one hundred percent finish. When the wood has been cleaned up, smear a little PVA glue on the spacers, bring all four bits of ply together, as illustrated, then leave the whole works in a clamp for at least twenty-four hours.

When the glue is dry, have a trial fitting, just to be sure that the body cavity is large enough to take the wheel, then set about drilling the pivotal dowel holes. Establish carefully the position of the three holes — that is to say the hole at the centre of the wheel, and the two holes through the body side plates, and then to work. Use the ¼ inch drill bit, and a scrap ply waster in the body cavity, then drill holes that are well placed and square with the working face of the ply. This done, have another trial fitting, but this time put the leg-wheel and washers within the cavity, then tap home the hardwood dowel.

Clean out the wheel pivotal hole, rub back the six feet, and generally make-good, until the wheel is a snug, nicely turning fit within the body.

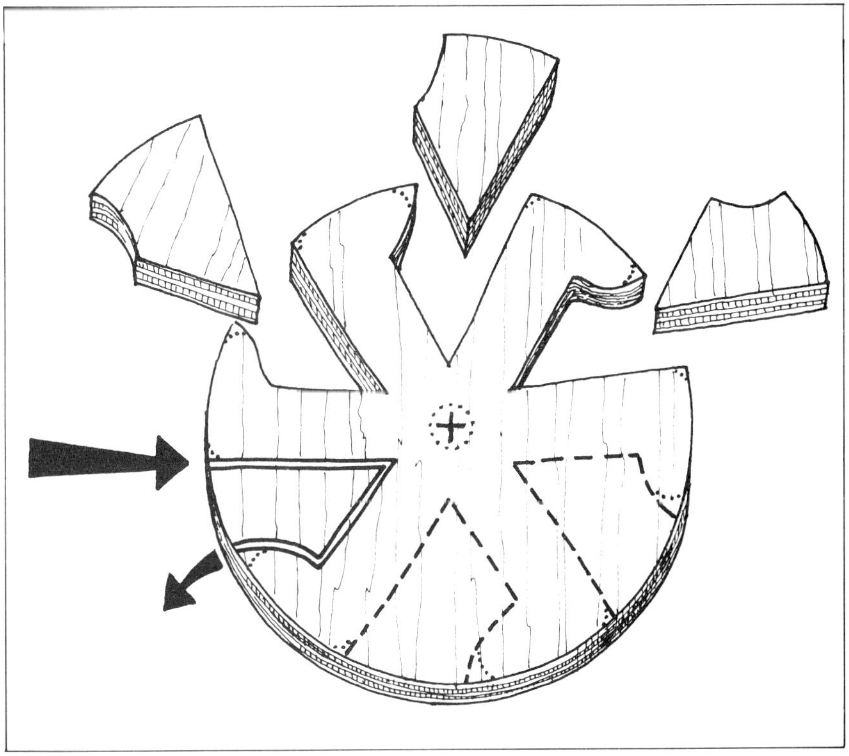

*When you have transferred the lines of the design to the wood, take the coping saw and very carefully cut away the between-leg wedges.*

## PAINTING

When you are happy with the fitting, knock out the dowel, then set out your painting areas so that all the tools and materials are to hand. Decide how you are going to support the wood while it is being painted — that is to say, are you going to hang it on threads, spike it on wires or some such; then stir and mix the paints. Now bearing in mind that the paint must dry out and be rubbed down between coats, lay on a primer, an undercoat, and a topcoat.

When the top gloss ground coat is completely dry, take a fine point brush and a selection of good strong colours and pick out all the decorative details — the plaid coat, the buttons, the hat, etc. Finally, when you reckon that the

*When the ply blank has been cut out, take a stick-tool supported piece of sandpaper and rub down all the cut edges until they are crisp and well rounded.*

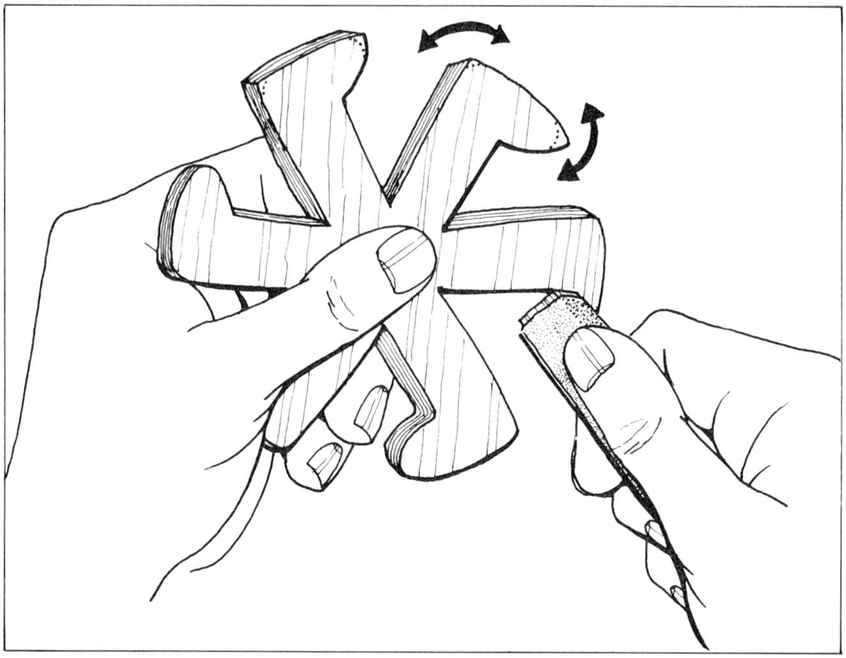

design has gone as far as it's going, then call a halt, wash and clean your brushes, and let the paint dry.

*Smear a little PVA glue on the various layers, build up the 'sandwich' in the correct order, and then put the whole works in a clamp.*

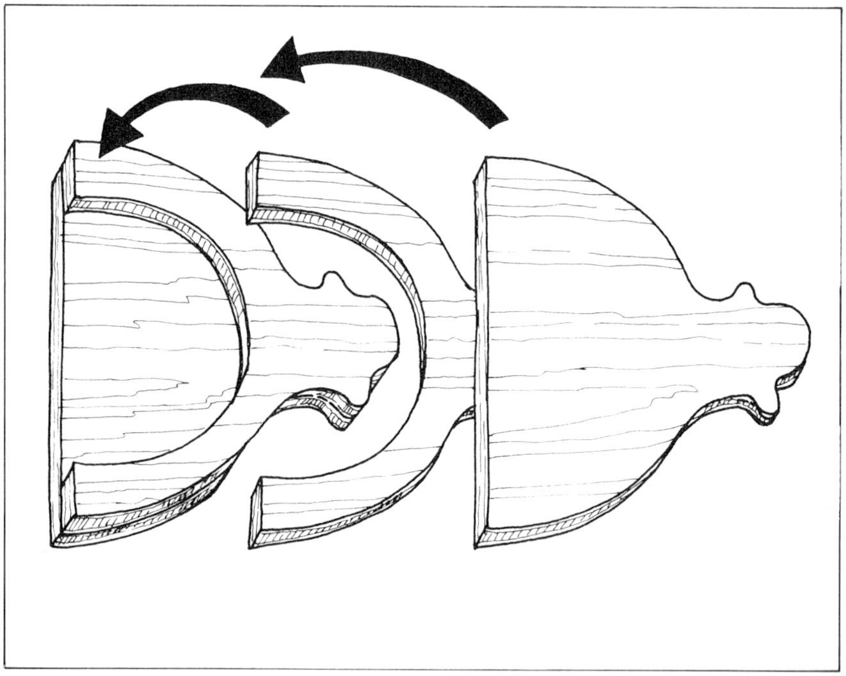

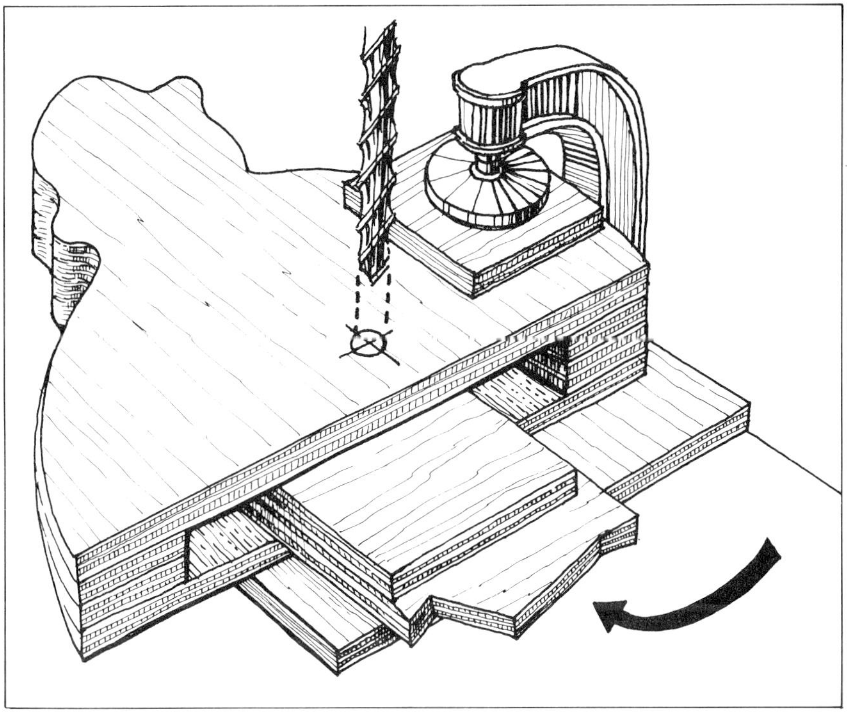

*When the glue is dry, pack out the body cavity with scrap wood, and then work the pivot hole. Note – it's very important that the hole be well placed, so check and double check, and make sure that the drill is at right angles to the working face of the wood.*

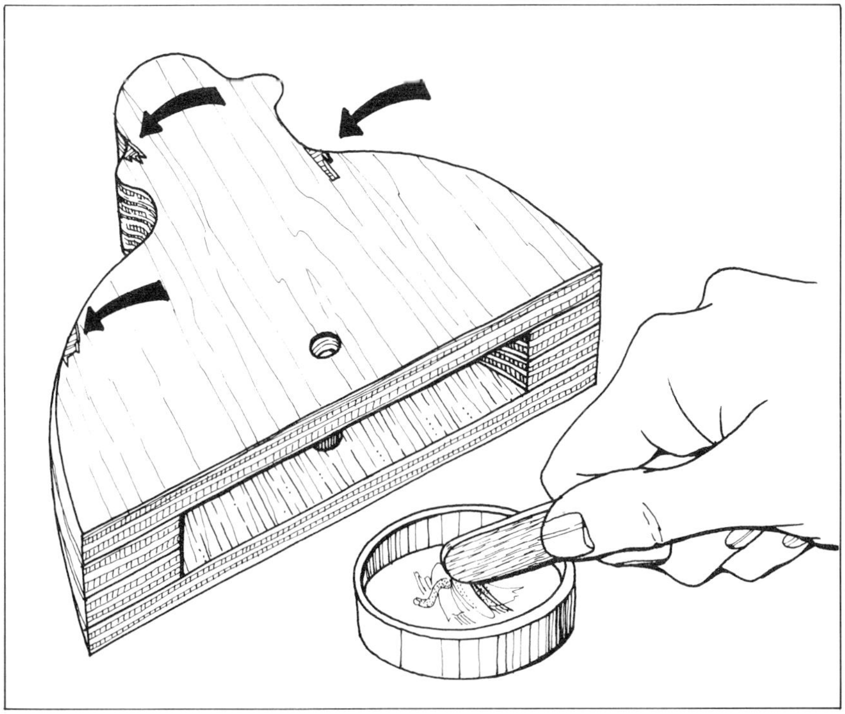

*Prior to painting and rubbing down, fill any breaks and tears with a resin/hardener car body filler.*

*When the man has been well rubbed down and painted, pick out the fine details with slender pointed brush. See how we use little wire hooks to handle and hang the wet pieces.*

## PUTTING TOGETHER

When the paint has dried, and you are sure that there are no blobs or tacky lumps, be ready with the dowel, washers, glue, saw and knife. First clean out

*When you come to putting the man together, slide the legs up into the body cavity, place and position the washers, then finally slide the dowel home and fix with a couple of dabs of PVA glue.*

the wheel hole, making certain that it's loose fit on the ¼ inch dowel, then put the body, washers and wheel in the correct 'sandwiched' order, as illustrated. Now tap home the dowel, check that the wheel spins smoothly, then glue the dowel ends, cut back for a flush finish, and the job is done.

## AFTERTHOUGHTS

When you are setting out the design, bear in mind that you do have to work the saw blade in and around the drawn shapes — go for a spacing that is economical and yet practical.

If you think that the six legged wheel needs to be a bit stronger, and say ½ inch thick, take account of paint thicknesses, and rub back the ply thickness to ⅜ inches.

If you want to make sure that the dowel is going to stay put, work a wedged-tenon, that is you cut the dowel to length, cut a dowel-end slot, then glue, wedge and trim.

Of course you might want to change the toy image to say a Milkmaid, a Mildred or a Man-Eating Monster — no matter, as long as the six-legged wheel is not too fragile — keep the legs short and strong.

When you have done with the painting area, put up 'Wet Paint' signs, then friends, family and literate pets won't blunder about and upset hours of work.

*The little man is 'walked' by gently rolling his legs on a carpet.*

PROJECT TWO

# THE SEGMENTAL SNAKE

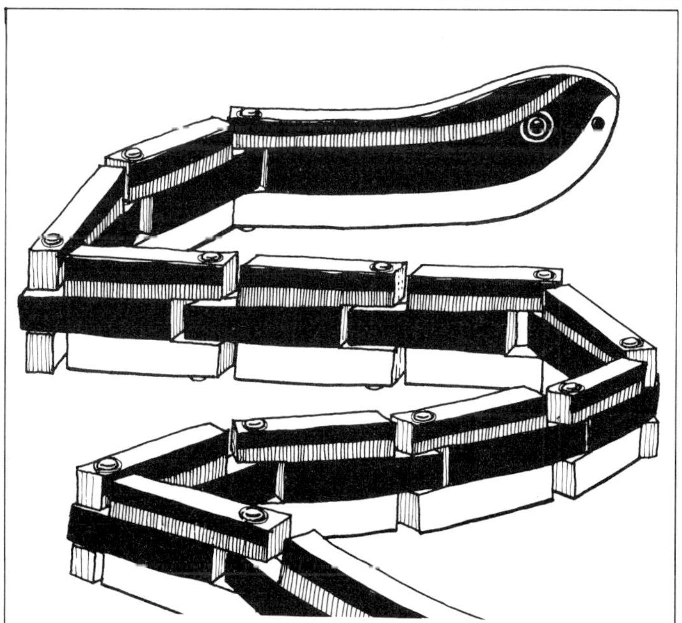

TOY TYPE · SEGMENTAL, HINGED AND BRIDLE - JOINTED

## THOUGHTS ON THE PROJECT

Snake and serpent toys have always been a favourite with children; little, surprise, Jack-in-the-box type snakes wriggling out of Japanese paper eggs; beautifully made, very realistic twisting and squirming, wood and leather snakes from China, and of course there are the modern, ever popular, 'trick' joke-shop rubber snakes. Show a group of children any sort of toy snake, and almost immediately they will express their love-hate feelings by screaming, giggling or wanting to touch. And of course this love-hate relationship that most of us have goes back a long way — what about this little gem from

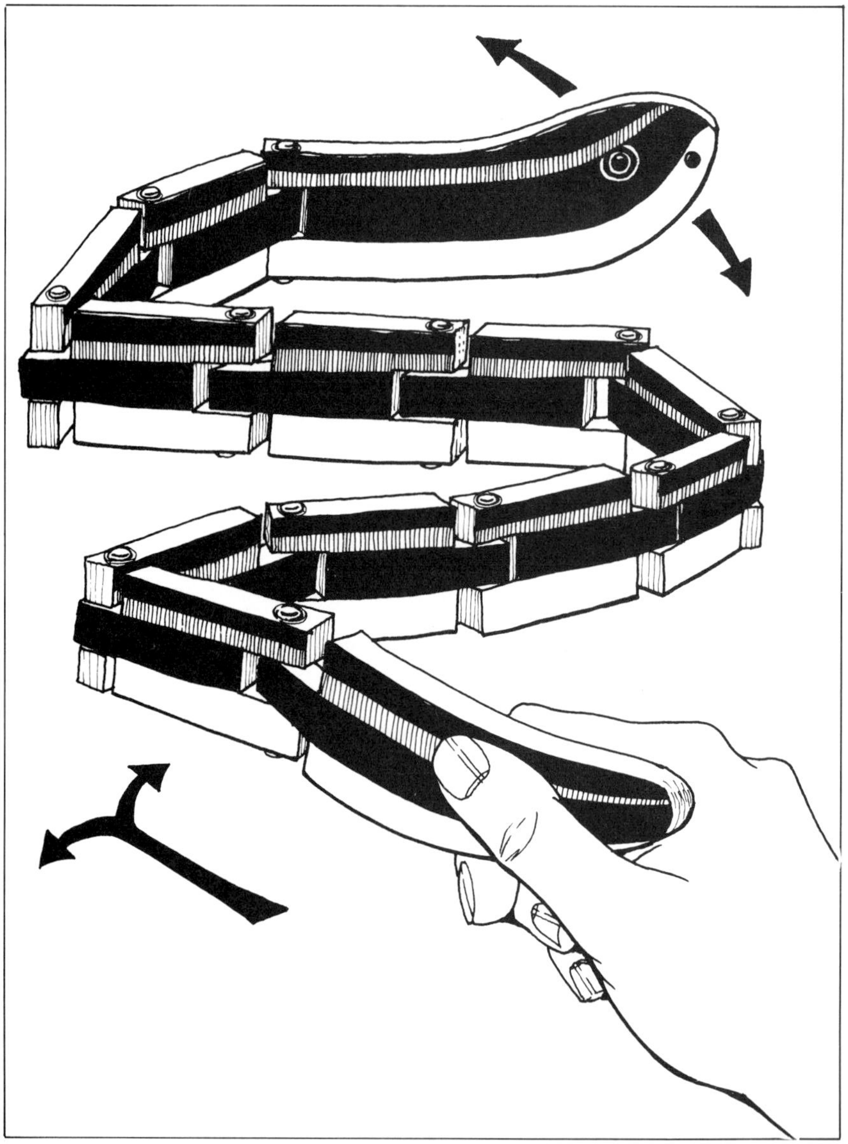

*In use, the snake is held by the tail, tilted up slightly and then very gently swung from side to side — the movement is quite wriggly and sinuous.*

Genisis . . . 'A curse on you of all creatures! a curse on you of all beasts! On your belly shall you crawl and eat dust all your days!' Poor old serpent! . . . what a life. Well not so with our toy snake, he's especially favoured – hold him up by his tail and straightaway he starts to writhe in a beautifully snaky way. 'Eeeeerh!' . . . 'Eeeek!'. We can almost hear the children enjoying this toy.

Now our segmented snake (we've not called him Sid, Sam or Cecil, because we can't afford to alienate any of our book-buying friends) has a shady, difficult to track down ancestry. Okay so he does maybe look a little like a

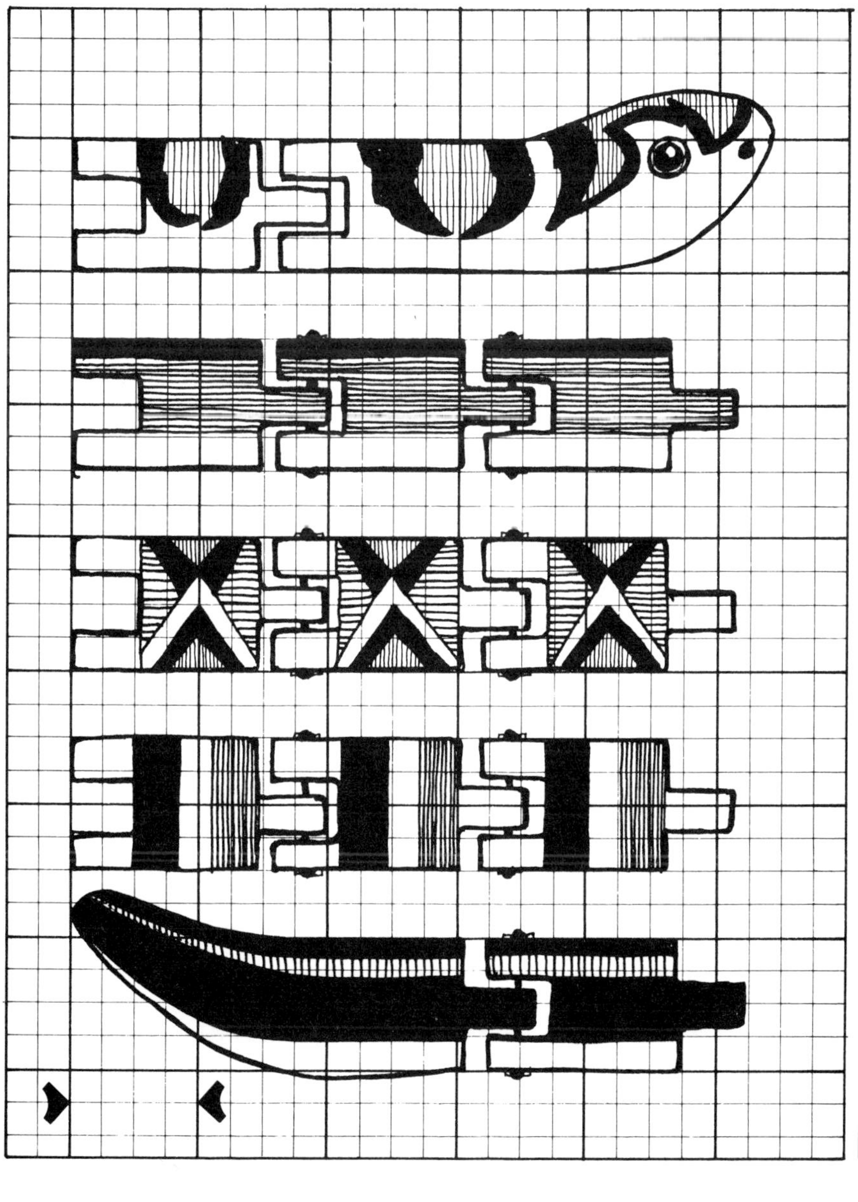

*Working Drawing, painting grid – note the scale of four squares to one inch. We show several possible ways of decorating the snake – see how each unit is painted before they are assembled.*

*Working Drawing, cutting grid – note the scale of four squares to one inch. There are eleven identical body units, and a head and tail – see how the mortise and tenon type bridle joint is a loose almost sloppy fit – this is as it should be.*

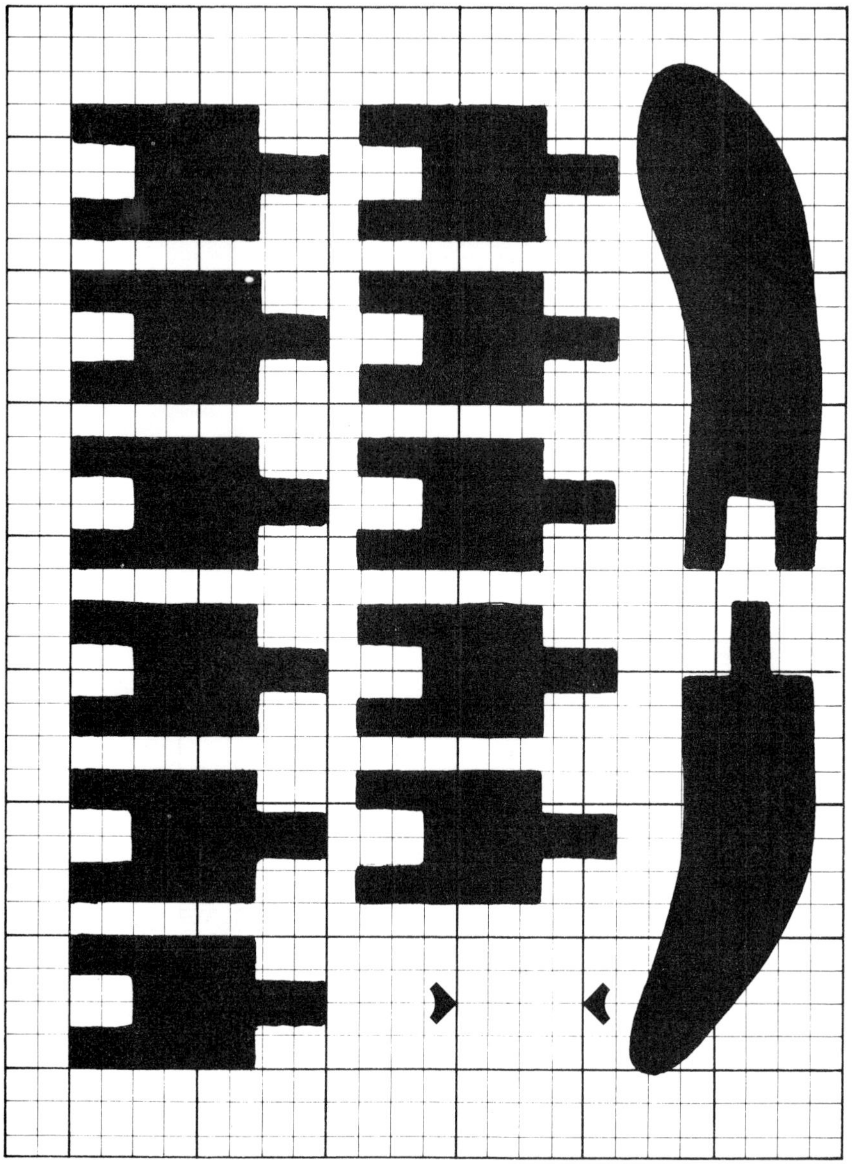

plastic segmented snake that was being sold in the shops a Christmas or two ago, and yes he reminds us of an Oriental wooden snake that a friend has, but as to belonging to a definite ethnic or folk toy tradition – who knows? All we can say with any confidence is that this snake was inspired by hazy memories of a 1940's/50's toy that we think we saw in a shop window. It's not much to go on, but no matter, this toy is a beauty, and we're sure his wormlike, squiggly, squirming, wriggly, sinuous movement will delight children and adults alike.

## CONSIDERING THE PROJECT

Before you start this project, take a piece of scrap paper and a pencil, then have a good look at our working drawings and note the scale, the number of body segments, and the pivotal, bridle joint hinge fixing. See how there are thirteen ¼ inch thick, multiply elements in all — a tail, a head and eleven identical, open mortise-and-tenon, bridle jointed segments. The scale, four squares to one inch, results in a snake that is about 25 inches long. If you, on consideration, want the snake to be shorter, fatter, broader or whatever,

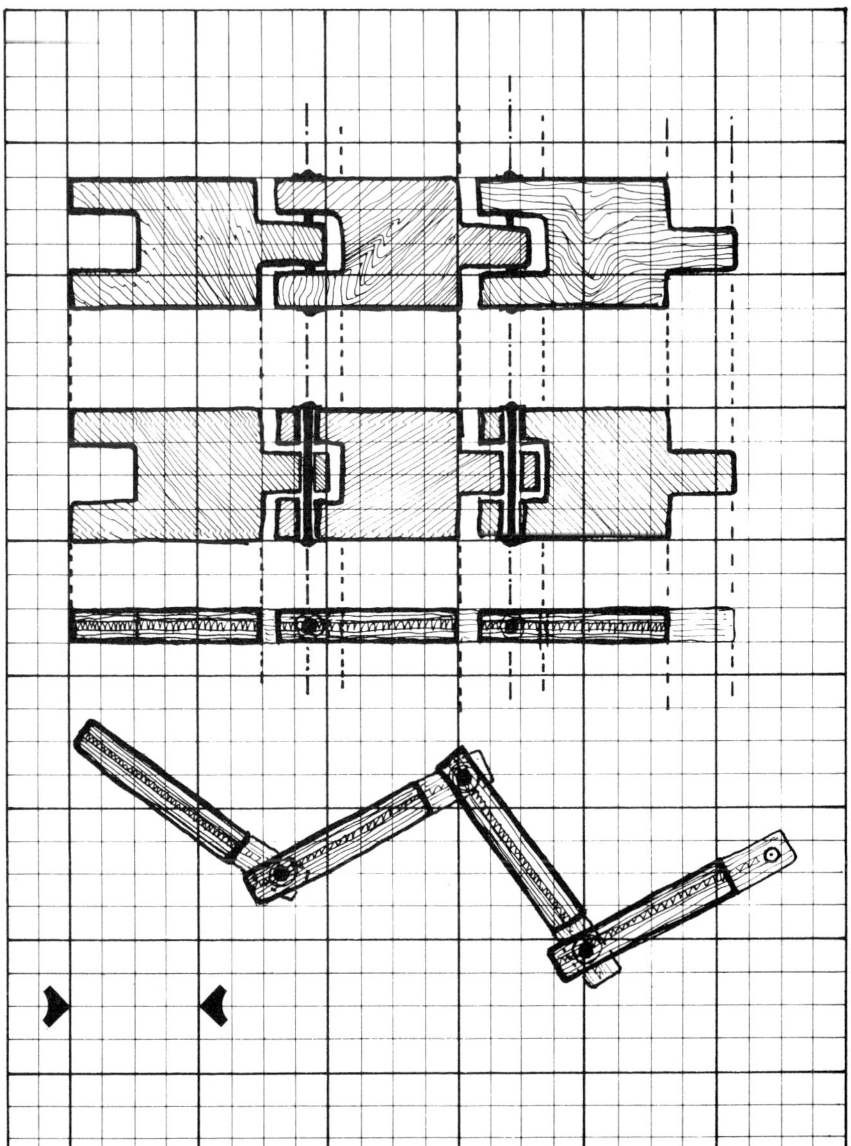

*Working Drawing, assembly grid – note the scale of four squares to one inch. We have used rivet pins and washers for the pivotal fixings, but you might use dowels, squash-end rods or whatever. Before you drill the pivot holes, make sure that the body units are so placed that they can swing back on themselves.*

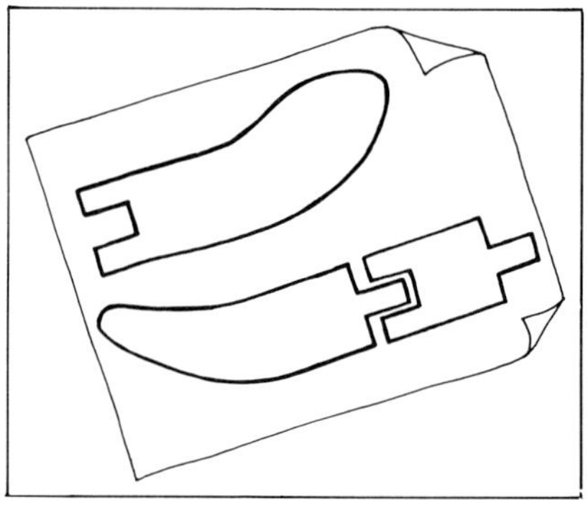

*Trace the head, the tail and a single body unit.*

now's the time to adjust the design. See also, before you spend out on materials, how we have pivot hinged the bridle joints with copper dome-end rivet pins, and then consider whether or not you want to modify our design and have say slender brass bolts, brass split pins, or some sort of patent rod-and-crimp-cap fixing.

Finally, study our rather bold and basic folk inspired suggestions for painting the snake, and decide just how you want your snake to be decorated; maybe you could take a trip to the nearest folk or toy museum and see if you can pick up one or two novel design and technique pointers.

## MATERIALS

For this project you need a piece of white faced ¼ inch multiply that measures about 7×12 inches, twelve ⅛ inch diameter soft copper, 1¼ inches long, dome head rivets, or maybe you could make your own, in which case you would need about 17 inches of soft copper wire; you need twenty-four brass washers to fit the rivets and finally you need a selection of model makers paints, plus of course wood primer and undercoat.

## TOOLS

As for tools, you need the use of a bench vice or table/bench holdfast, a coping or fret saw with a pack of spare blades, a hand drill with a ⅛ inch drill bit, a light ball-ended hammer, pliers, a small hack-saw. a flat model makers file, a pack of graded sandpapers, a selection of stick-tools, a sharp knife or ½ inch chisel, a metal ruler, and finally you need such items as pencils, tracing paper, brushes and acres of scrap workout paper.

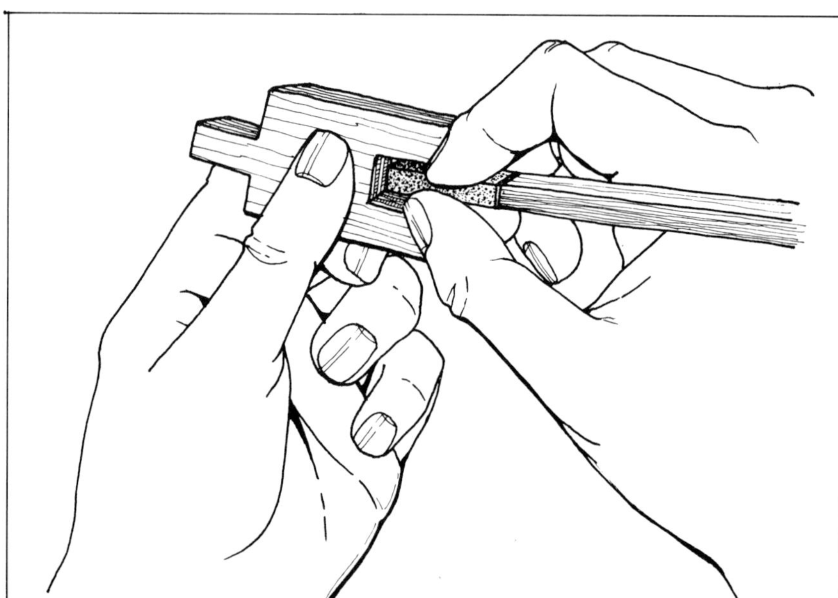

*Cut out the drawn shapes with a coping saw, then take the wood to a good finish with a stick-tool and sandpaper. Rub off all burrs, and make sure that all the cut ply edges are smooth to the touch.*

## SETTING OUT THE DESIGN

Before you put saw to wood, consider just how clever, or not so clever you are with a coping saw, and then adjust and modify the cutting of the hinged bridle joints accordingly. For example, if you are able to saw a tight fine line, then you might want to cut the eleven identical open mortise-and-tenon body sections from a couple of 12 × 1 inch lengths of ply; this would mean that you would be working both halves of the bridle joint in a single cut, rather as you would if you were fretting out a jigsaw puzzle. On the other hand, if you are a raw beginner you might prefer to work a little, step at a time, and say cut eleven 2 × 1 inch pieces, and then cut each and every piece with its own head-and-tail profile.

We have chosen to go for the 'beginner' way of working. Start by taking a pencil, ruler and workout paper, and drawing to size the head, the tail, and just one of the body sections. This done, check that the open tenon is going to be a good loose fit in the mortise, then pencil press transfer the lines of the design through to the working face of the ply. Note – you will of course have to keep repeating the body section transference until you have eleven identical units.

## CUTTING, DRILLING AND RUBBING DOWN

When you have drawn out and established all thirteen shapes, sit back, and check that there are twelve mortises, twelve tenons, and that the snake's head starts with a mortise, and the tail finishes with a tenon. Now put the wood in the vice, take up the coping saw and cut out all the drawn shapes. Don't worry, at this stage, about the joints, just fret out the overall shape. The

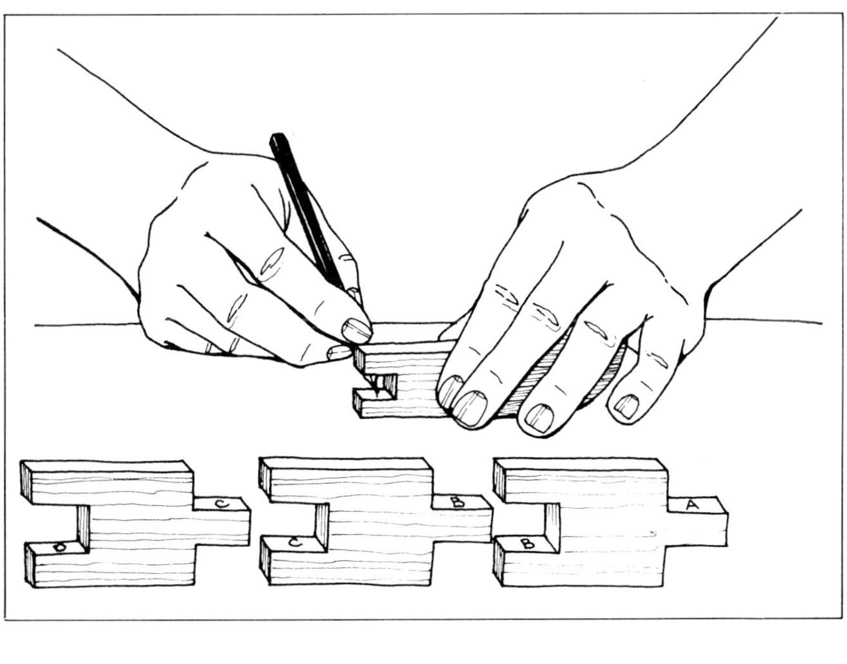

*Prior to drilling and painting, mark all the body bridle joints, so that each and every part is individually matched.*

*When you come to drilling the pivotal holes, place matched body units in the vice, then take the 1/8 inch drill bit and work the holes right through the joint. Note – it is most important that the holes are well placed and aligned, so 'sight' up and hold the drill so that it enters and leaves the wood at right angles.*

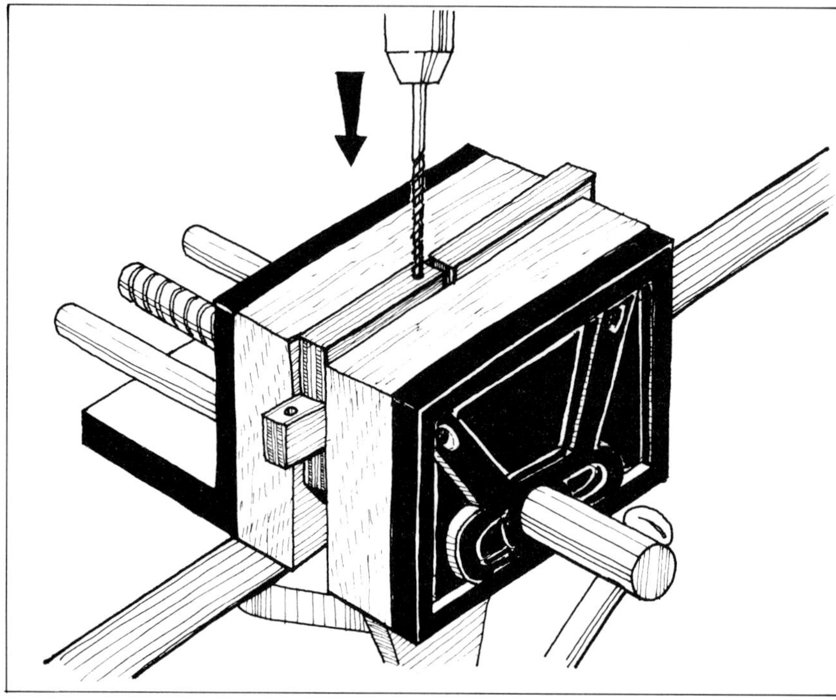

snake's head needs to be about 4 inches long, the tail about 3–4 inches long, and eleven body parts each at 2 inches.

Now, working a part at a time, take the saw and cut out the various tenon and mortise profiles. Note that the mortise should be ½ inch wide and ½ inch deep, where as the tenon should be a little under ½ inch wide, and a little over ½ inch in length – see the working drawings and section details. This done arrange all the bridle-cut shapes out on the worksurface so that you have a continuous head-to-tail snake form that is ¼ inch thick, 1 inch wide and about 25 inches long. When you are sure that all is correct, take a pencil and go along the snake labelling the matching joints, A–A, B–B, C–C and so on.

Now, starting at one end or other, it makes no matter, take up the ply shapes two-by-two, put them in the vice, and then drill and work the 1/8 inch pivotal holes, as illustrated. Finally, when all the joints have been cut and drilled, and you have checked them over for hole alignment, take knife or chisel and sandpaper, and work all the edges, corners and cuts to a well rounded smooth finish. Note – to a certain extent each matched and drilled joint is individual, so don't lose sight of the labelling.

## PAINTING

When all thirteen parts of the snake have been well prepared, and bearing in mind that between coats the paint needs to be dried and rubbed down, lay on a primer, an undercoat, a topcoat and the final decorative detailing. Now, with the distinguishing labelling, or colour coding still intact, put the pieces to one side until the paint is completely dry.

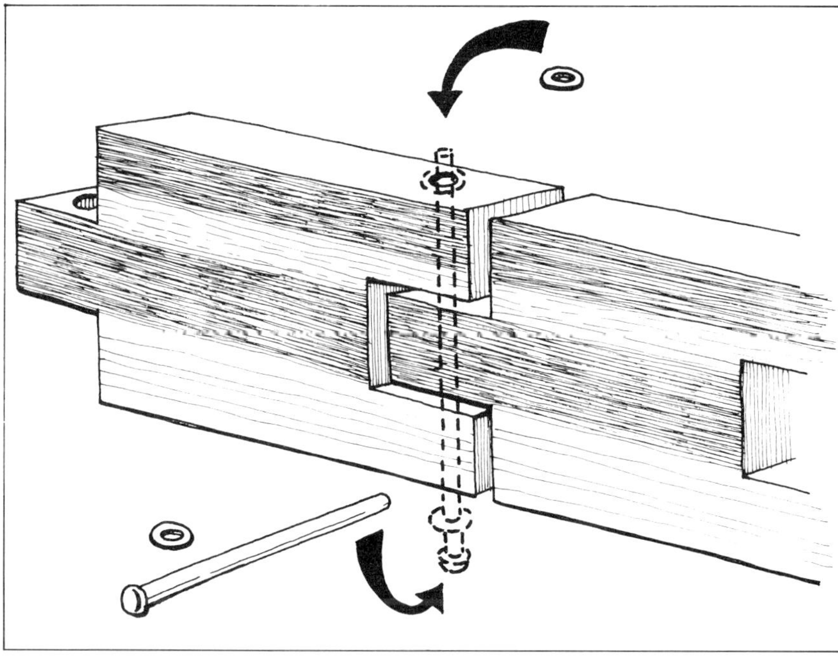

*When all the units have been well worked and prepared, position the washers and slide home the rivet pin. Note – the wood is prepared and painted before being riveted; we've not shown the painted motifs on this illustration because they obscure the details.*

## PUTTING TOGETHER

When the paint is dry, set the snake out in its correct order, then be ready with the copper rivets, the brass washers, the pliers and the hammer. A word

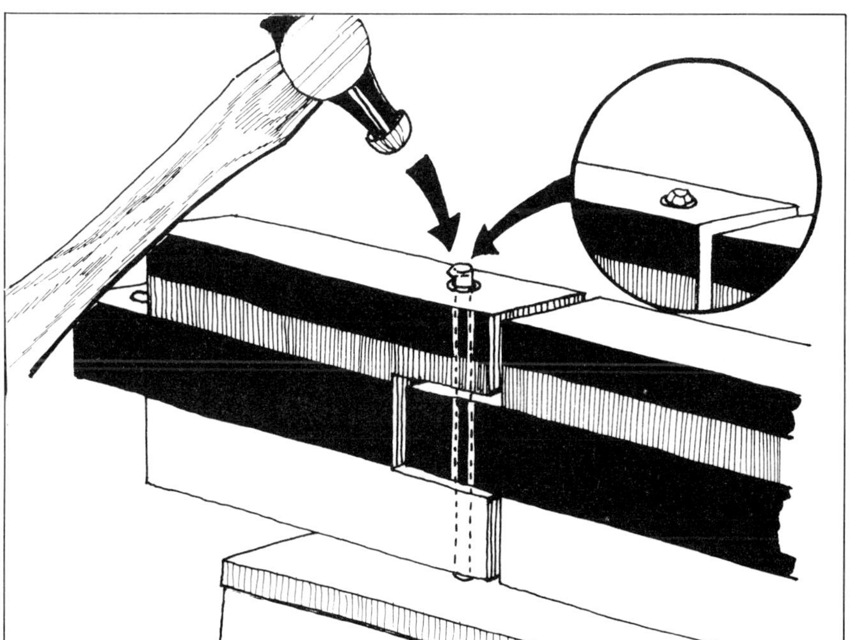

*And so, unit by unit, you place the rivet pins and washers – support the rivet head down on an iron block, then take a pin hammer and gently tap over the tail of the rivet. Don't be too heavy handed with the hammer, just work the rivet tail with a series of glancing blows until it's dome-headed against the washer.*

of caution — without doubt the riveting is tricky, so work at it slowly, and maybe have a trial run with some scrap. Take up a matched pair of shapes, link the joint with two washers and a copper rivet, as illustrated, then hold the unit so that the rivet head is supported head-down on say an iron block or the heel of a metalwork vice.

Now take a round faced or ball hammer and tap over the tail of the rivet with a dozen or so gentle, well placed glancing blows. Don't attempt to beat and clinch the rivet, but rather just aim to work it until the tail is rounded against the washer. And so you continue, until you have fixed all twelve bridle joints.

Finally, go over the rivet heads with a file, just to make sure that they are smooth and free from burrs and sharp edges; then take a fine-point brush, and a dab or two of paint, and go along the snake making good any scratches or chips.

## AFTERTHOUGHTS

At about 25 inches long, this toy is a sensitive, delicate, fragile plaything suitable for older children, however if you want a sturdier toy, then there is no reason at all why you shouldn't use a heavier ply, and reduce the number of body units to say five or six.

If you decide to use brass pins for the joints (as an easy option) bear in mind that in time these pins will work loose, fall out, and become a hazard to 'suck-everything' infants.

When you are drilling the pivotal holes, make sure that they are square to the ply, and well back from the end of the tenon.

When you are sanding down the wood, prior to painting, be sure to rub off all the corners in-and-around the bridle joints, and then have a dry fitting to make sure the joint swings freely. If you don't like the idea of rivets, you can use thicker ply for the snake's body and use wooden dowels; or you can use a patent cap-end fixing, or, if you are handy with a soldering gun, you can have washers and 'blob-end' copper pins.

PROJECT THREE

# THE MUZHIK AND THE BEAR

TOY TYPE · PARALLEL RODS AND PIVOTAL FIGURES

## THOUGHTS ON THE PROJECT

For some years now we've known this toy as 'The Bear and The Woodcutter', and thought of it as belonging to the Groden Valley tradition of woodcarved toys; that is to say toys made in the eighteenth and nineteenth century in Austria and Germany. However after a great many week-ends spent sniffing around in museums and old bookshops, we have come to the conclusion that in fact this toy doesn't illustrate a woodcutter, but rather it shows a Russian Muzhik blacksmith and a bear (muzhik, moujik or mujik, meaning a peasant under the tzars). Now better still, another little snippet of information has come our way that suggests that not only does this toy have its roots in an old Russian folk tale about a blacksmith and a bear, but toys of just this character and design are still being made by woodcarvers in the central Russian, Volga Basin town of Bogorodsk. Of course the Russian folk-rustic woodcarvers no longer whittle away in their own isolated 'woodcutter' cottages; instead they now work in semi mass production co-operatives, much as the English 'New Forest' carver toymakers did in the 1920's and 1930's.

However, all that apart, the 'Muzhik and the Bear' belong to the centuries old tradition of simple, folk-made, woodcarved mechanical automata, and as such it is considered to be an archetypal toy classic. The strong simple-movement construction is both basic and exciting – give the parallel sticks a backwards-and-forwards jerk, and in turn the two figures hammer or chop away. A beautiful thought provoking noisy toy – just perfect for active enquiring toddlers.

## CONSIDERING THE DESIGN

Although with this project, we have stayed with the overall feel of the Muzhik and the bear, we have updated the man, changed him to a woodcutter and given him a stylized lumberjack image. Of course there is no reason at all why you shouldn't go for two non-traditional images. We've seen this toy set out as wrestlers, clowns, birds, boxers, a fish and fisherman, and so on – as long as the sticks are parallel and both figures squarely pivoted, then the simple movement can be achieved.

And then again, if you look at the working drawings and details, you will see that the figures have flat side panels, laminated spacers and flat sticks, all being made out of 3/16 inch multiply. As long as the two figures can sit loosely astride the parallel sticks, then there is no reason why you shouldn't say, use thinner or thicker wood, use several ply types and thicknesses, build out and carve the figures to give them a 'fatter' more realistic image, or whatever. Our grid scale of four squares to one inch give a stick-end to stick-end measurement of about six inches, and a total figure height of about three inches.

Finally, at this point in the project, it is a good idea to visit toy museums, and then to sit back with workout paper, a ruler and pencil, and see if you can come up with a uniquely exciting design.

## MATERIALS

For this project you need a piece of top quality white faced 3/16 inch multiply

*Working Drawing, painting grid – note the scale of four squares to one inch. Keep the painted design bold and simple with plenty of bright colours and clear-cut graphic shapes.*

that measures about 6×8 inches, four 1 inch long, ¼ inch diameter, hardwood dowels, or patent, clip-end, metal pins; eight brass washers to fit your chosen pivots, a quantity of white PVA wood glue, a selection of model makers paints, and a white wood primer and undercoat to suit the paints.

**Tools** As for tools you need the use of a bench vice or bench holdfast, a fine bladed fret or coping saw, plus of course a pack of spare blades, a hand drill with a ¼ inch drill bit, a selection of shaped stick-tools plus a pack of graded sandpapers, a small sharp knife, and as with all the other projects you need all the usual house and workshop tools and items like pencils, brushes, rulers, scraps of wood, throw-away tubs, and such like.

## SETTING OUT THE DESIGN

Have a good look at our working drawings and details, and see how the toy has been broken down so that there are ten ply cut-outs in all — two woodcutter side plates, two woodcutter spacers, two bear side plates, two bear spacers and two sticks. Now decide just how you want your toy to be, its

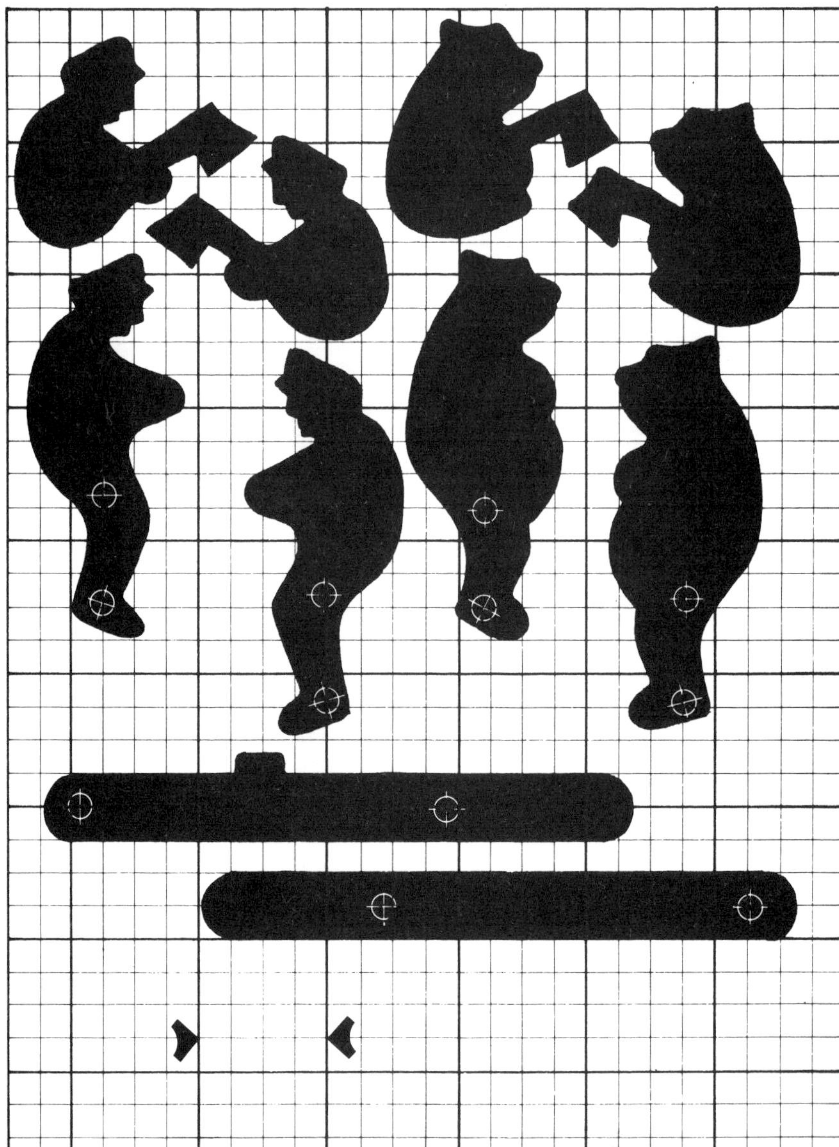

*Working Drawing, cutting grid – note the scale of four squares to one inch. There should be ten cut-ply shapes in all: two man side plates, two man spacers, two bear side plates, two bear spacers and two sticks. Note the position of all the pivotal holes – it's most important that they be well placed.*

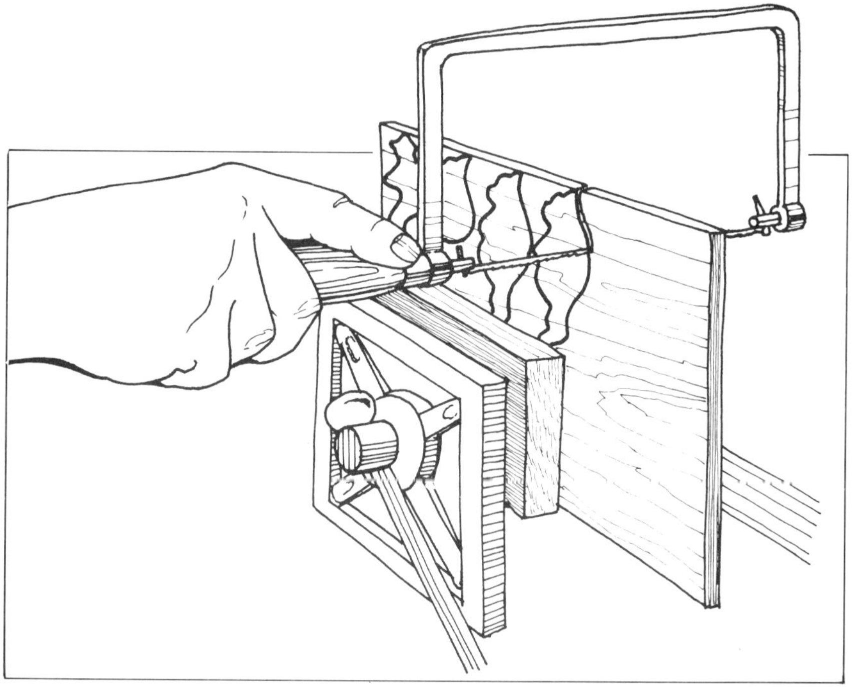

*When you have transferred the traced design to the working face of the wood, cut out the shapes with a coping saw – see how the saw blade is at right angles to the face of the wood.*

size and design, then take your workout paper and work the patterns to size. This done, carefully trace your master design, then pencil press transfer the lines of the design through to the working face of the ply. Now pencil in and establish the transferred lines, then label the various drawn shapes so that you are sure as to their function and placing in the scheme of things.

When you are happy with the pattern, place the wood in the vice, take up the coping saw, and then to work. Cut and manoeuvre the blade and the wood so that the cutting line comes outside the drawn line, and be very careful, especially when you are sawing against the grain, that you don't rip or tear the working face of the ply.

## PLACING, GLUING AND LAMINATING

When all your ply shapes have been fretted out, stop awhile, have a look at the working drawings, then set out the cut forms so that they make up the two figures. Note the total wood thickness of $^{3}/_{4}$ inch. When you reckon that all is correct, smear the ply with PVA glue, then place the glued-up 'sandwich' in a clamp and leave it be for twenty-four hours.

## DRILLING, RUBBING DOWN AND PAINTING

When the glue is dry, check with all your workouts, working drawings, inspirational illustrations and notes, then set out all your tools so that they are to hand. Start off by carefully establishing the position of the pivot points, then, using scrap ply wasters, as illustrated, work the various drilled holes. Now with this toy, it's most important that the pivotal holes be square to the working face of the wood, so pay particular attention to the angle at which the drill bit enters the wood. Note – if you don't use the wasters between the figure side plates, there is a chance that the drill will tear and damage the surface ply – work with extra caution. And so you continue, drilling the holes at the 'ankle', 'thigh' and through the sticks.

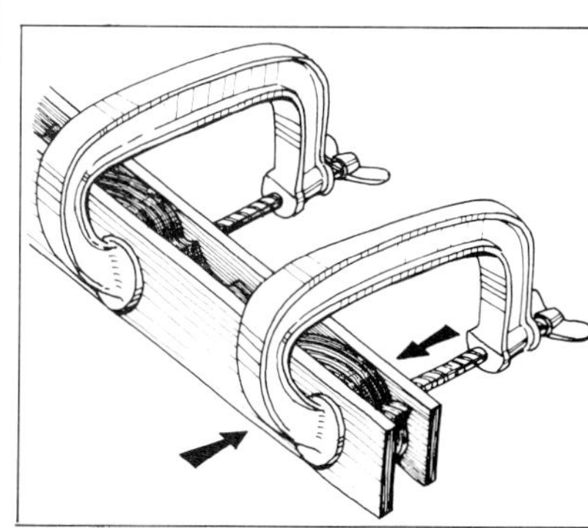

*Give the sawn shapes a swift rub down with sandpaper, then smear them with PVA glue, and then clamp them up, as shown in the working drawing sections.*

*Working Drawing, assembly grid – note the scale of four squares to one inch. At the 'still' position, that is with both little figures sitting upright, all the holes should be aligned and four-square, and the two sticks should be parallel. See how the leg/stick space needs to be packed out with washers, and how the dowels are a loose fit in the sticks and glued into the figures.*

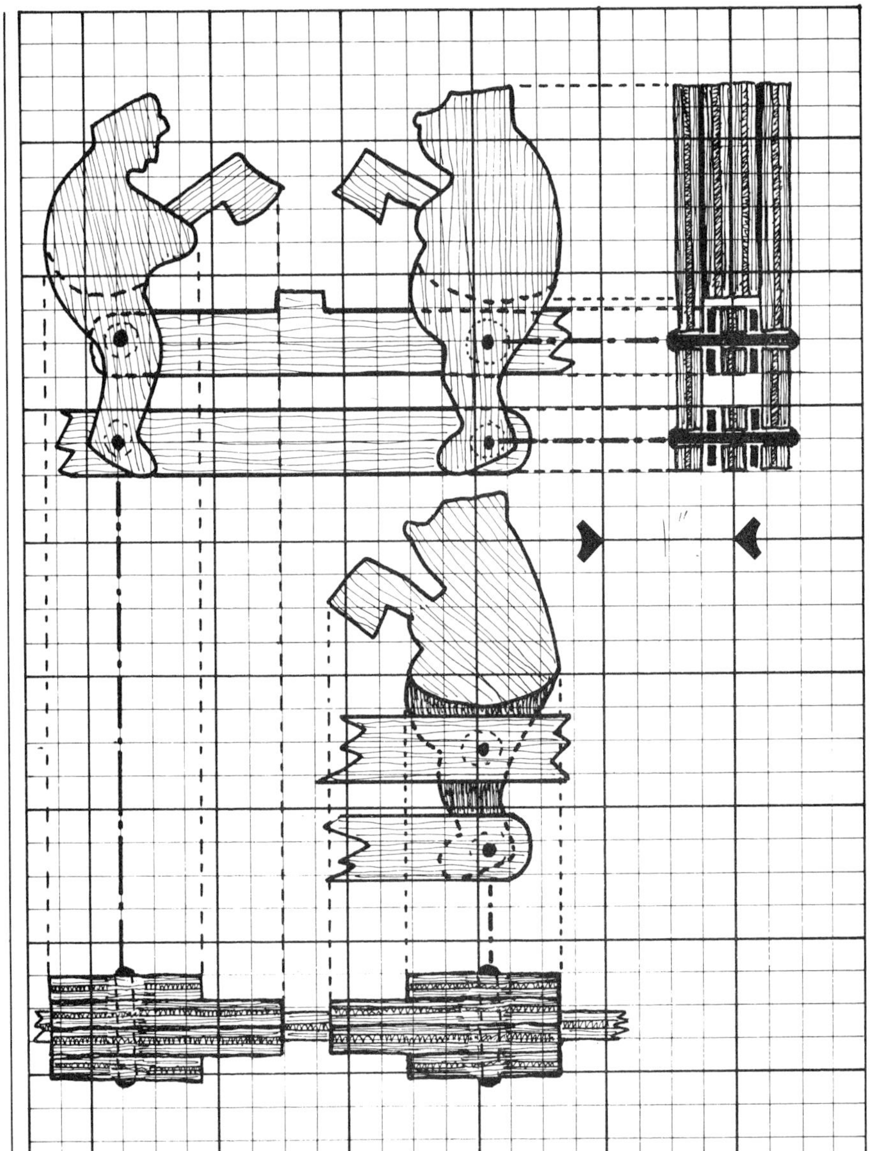

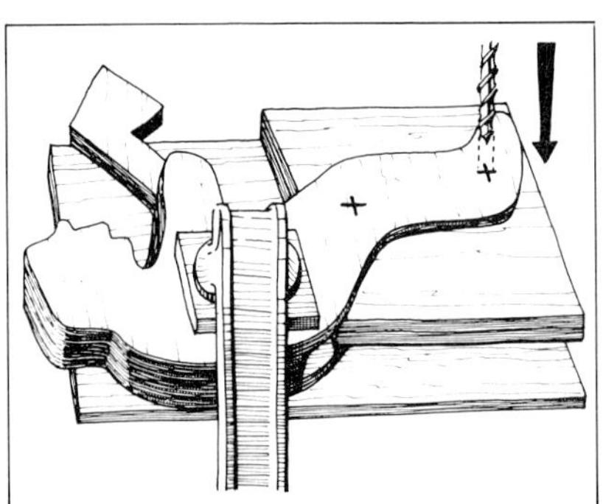

*When the glue is dry, establish the position of the pivotal holes, pack out the leg cavity with scrap wood, then set-to with the drill. See how the four thicknesses of ply go to make up the total figure.*

This done, take the pivotal rods and have a dry trial fitting – see how the figures sit astride the sticks, and how as you push-and-pull, the two little figures tilt, chop and bob. When you are sure that all's correct, smear a little resin filler in and on all edge tears, wait a few minutes for it to dry off, then take the graded sandpapers and stick-tools, and rub down to a good finish. Clean out the drilled holes; rub off all cut edges, and generally work away until all edges and corners are smooth, nicely profiled, rounded, and completely 'toddler-sucking' safe.

This done, wipe up all the wood dust with a damp cloth, take the prepared

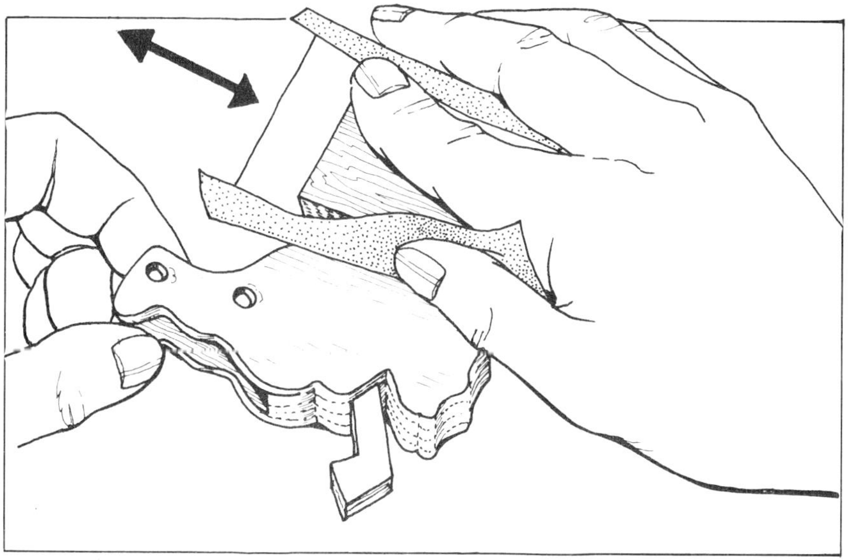

*When the holes have been worked, take some sandpaper and rub down the wood to a good smooth-edged finish.*

quality of the paints, the quality of the brushes, the painting environment, the amount of water vapour in the atmosphere, the temperature; all these factors can effect the finish. Our considered advice after many years of trial, error, and more than a few dismal upsets, is to take it very slowly, a step at a time — never mix paint types and brands — always let the paint dry out thoroughly between coats, and always go for several thin coats rather than a single corner-cutting flooding.

Finally, when you have achieved a good smooth gloss topcoat, take a fine-

*Paint the toy units, as described in other projects, then with dowel and washers fix the two figures astride their sticks. Finally, make sure all is correct, then tap home the glue-end dowels.*

*When the glue is dry, take a fine-point brush and just make good the dowel ends.*

shapes to your painting area, then set out the brushes, primer, undercoat, topcoat, cleaner and throw-away containers. Now lay on an even coat of primer, wait for it to dry, then take the fine sandpaper and rub back to a smooth finish. And so you continue, brushing on paint layers, letting them dry and then cutting back with the sandpaper until you have achieved a good topcoat finish.

Without doubt, painting is tricky — the type of wood to be painted, the

*In use, the two sticks are firmly held, then they are jiggled backwards and forwards so that the two figures take turns in striking the block.*

point long haired brush, and a selection of well stirred colours, and pick out all the little details of the eyes, face, shirt, trousers, stick pattern and such like. Keep these final details strong and firm — don't try for subtle 'true to life' blends of colour, or fussy brush strokes — just keep the shapes and motifs bold, and the brush strokes swift.

## BRINGING TOGETHER AND GLUING THE PIVOT RODS

When the paint is dry, clean out the holes in the two sticks, making sure that they are a loose fit on the ¼ inch dowels, then put the toy together as illustrated. The rods should go through a leg hole, through a brass washer, through the stick, through another washer, through the other leg, and finally come to rest in the other leg hole.

Finally, cut back the dowel ends with a knife, fix with a spot or two of PVA glue, dab the dowel ends with paint, and the job is done.

## AFTERTHOUGHTS

With this project, the placing of the pivotal holes is critical — get them ever so slightly off true, or out of alignment, and the sticks will jamb. If you want to precisely establish the hole positions, it's a good idea to make a card and pin working model or prototype.

If, when you are cutting the wood, you damage the edges or the working face, make-good with a hardener/resin type car-body filler — never use a cheap plaster filler.

PROJECT FOUR

# CHUCKY CHICK

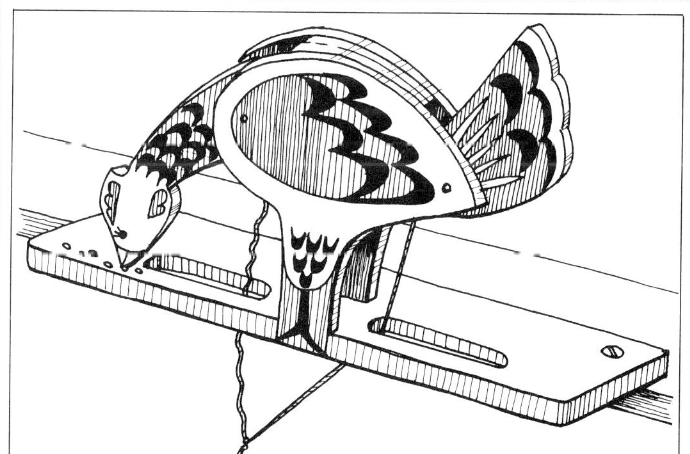

TOY TYPE · PIVOTAL, COUNTERBALANCE AND PENDULUM

## THOUGHTS ON THE PROJECT

This toy is a real beauty — fix its bracketed stand to a shelf edge or table top, set the pendulum swinging, and low and behold you have a chick that looks to be very realistically pecking at corn. We've seen dozens of such toys; that is with simple pendulum operated movement — everything from little carved and painted hens made in pre-war Russia and Austria, to a Dodo made in nineteenth century Ireland, and a Disney type dog made in the 1950's. These toys are simple to make and yet their life-like movement is ingenious and completely captivating.

Have a toy of this character fixed over a toddler's bed, or even, come to that, on a shelf edge in your kitchen or office, and it will give you and your family hours of fun. Of course as likely as not your friends will ask, 'How?' 'When?' and 'Where?' — all we can say is that this is a classic folk toy, but as to giving any historical background information, that's something again. European? American? Russian? — it's almost impossible to say, we've seen this toy described as 'a penny toy', 'an American Primitive', 'a nineteenth century English street toy', 'a German Woodcarved Toy', 'a Nuremberg and Wurtemberg Toy', 'a Czechoslovakian Mountain Toy', and so we could go on. No doubt, toys of just this type were made and peddled by European medieval toymakers — who knows? Enough to say that this toy is a real charmer and great fun — we reckon that be you eight, eighteen or eighty, you won't be able to keep a straight face when you see the chick's head and tail bobbing up and down.

## CONSIDERING THE DESIGN

If you stop awhile and look at our inspirational illustrations you will see that traditional toys of this character are usually designed so that they have a bracketed base complete with a large clamp screw and butterfly nut. We thought about using a shop-bought metal G-clamp, and we also considered showing you how to make a wooden screw-clamp, but in the end we settled for a simple design that has a firm base that can be screw-fixed or clamped as you so wish.

If you look at our drawings and grids you will see that they are worked to a grid scale of four squares to one inch — note also how we use ¼ inch multiply, and how the toy beak-to-tail measures about 6–7 inches. The actual movement and fixing is simple and straightforward, the head and tail being loosely pivoted within the body, and the pendulum strings being glued and plugged into the neck and the tail. When the pendulum is swung, the weight shifts backwards and forwards, and the head and tail both rock and nod on their hardwood pivots . . . very pretty?!

## MATERIALS

For this project you need a piece of top quality white faced ¼ inch multiply that measures about 9 × 9 inches, two 1 inch long ¼ inch diameter hardwood dowels, four brass washers to fit the dowels, half a dozen ½ inch brass pins, a quantity of PVA wood glue, a selection of best quality model makers paints, a white wood primer and undercoat to suit your chosen paints, about 36 inches

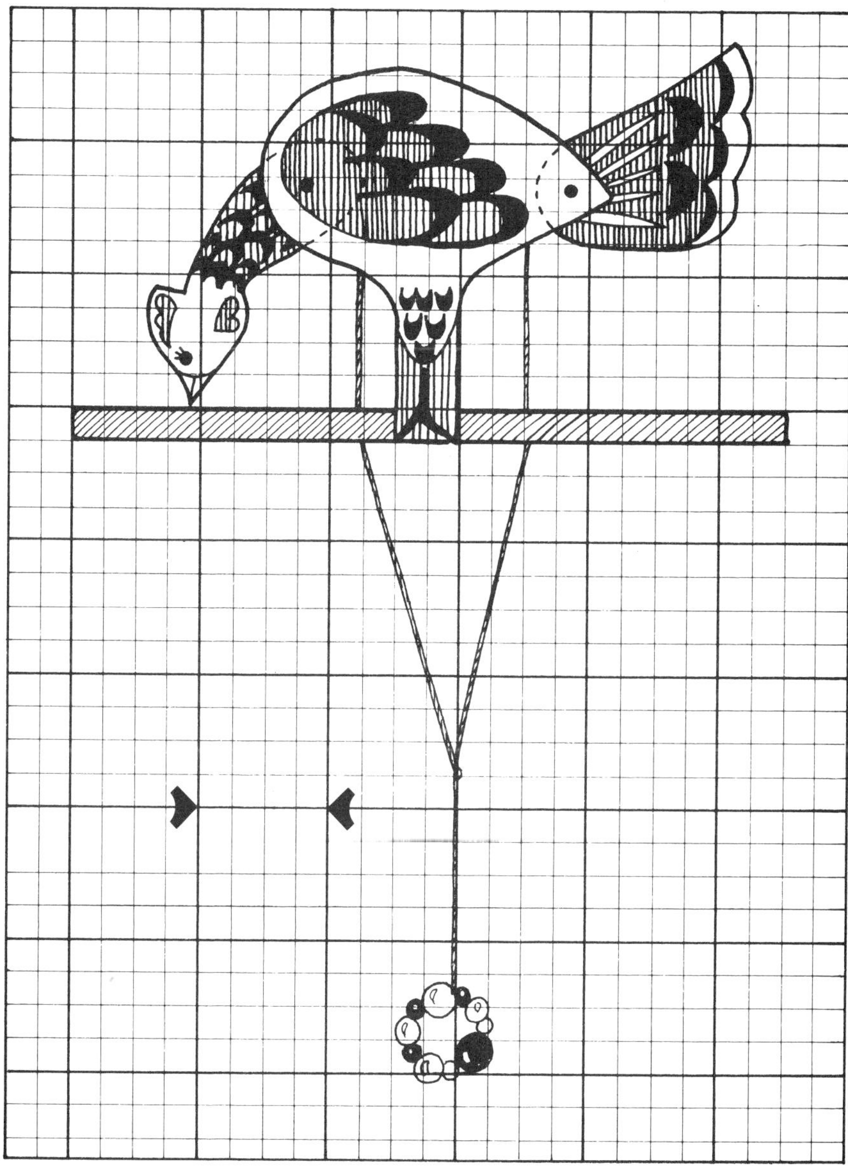

*Working Drawing, painting grid – note the scale of four squares to one inch.*

of fine cord and finally you will need a pendulum bob — we have used a collection of heavy glass and ceramic beads, but you might prefer a wooden ball, a cast fisherman's weight, a brass plumb-line bob or some such.

## TOOLS

You need the use of a bench vice or table clamp, a fine-blade coping saw, a small hand drill with a ¼ inch diameter drill bit, a selection of shaped stick-tools, a pack of graded sandpapers, work-out and tracing paper, a small

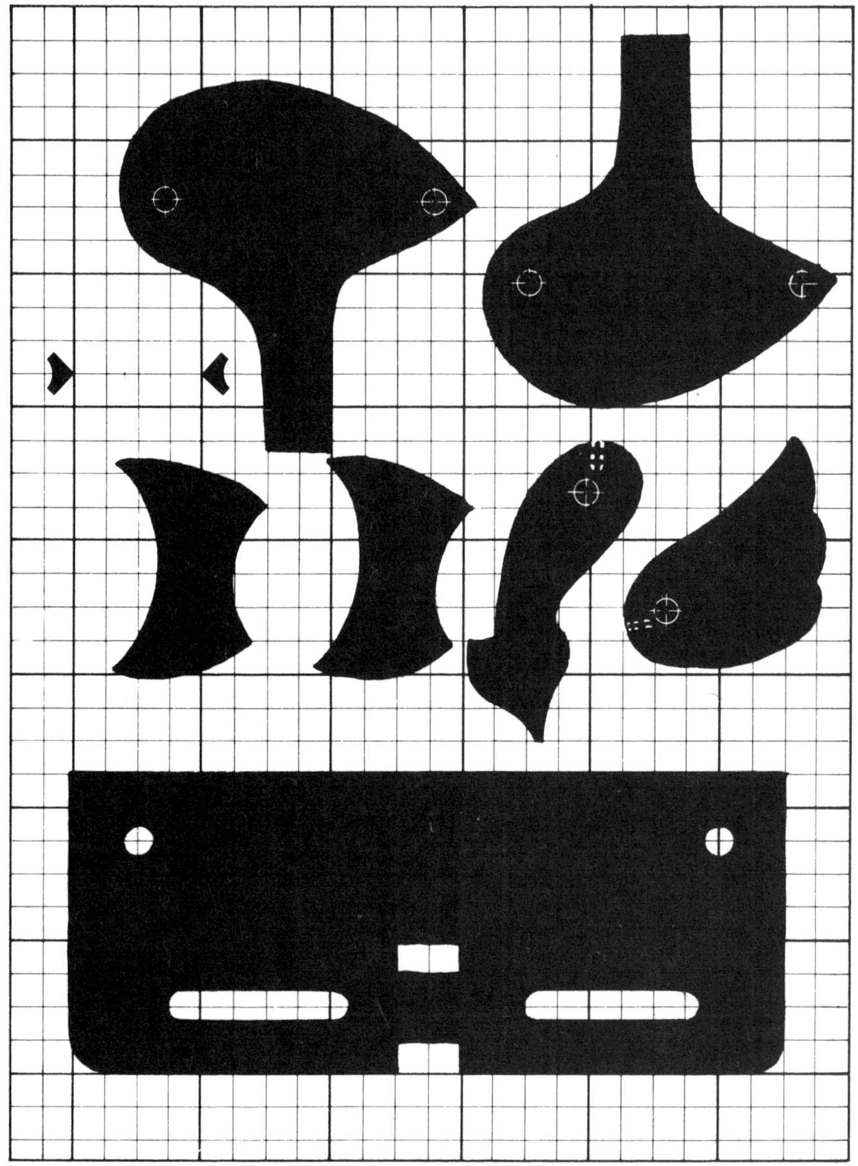

*Working Drawing, cutting grid – note the scale of four squares to one inch. There are seven shapes or units in all.*

chisel for the mortise, a small long-bladed knife, and finally you will need all the usual workshop tools like pencils, a metal ruler, brushes and a square.

## DESIGNING, SETTING-OUT AND CUTTING THE PLY

Have a good long look at our inspirational illustrations and gridded drawings, and see how we have worked the toy so that it is entirely made out of ¼ inch multiply. And of course at this stage, decide whether or not you want to modify our designs. This done, give your wood a thorough checking over just to make sure that it is completely free from flaws, then set out your work area so that all your tools and materials are to hand.

Now carefully trace the various toy elements, that is to say the two side body panels, the two body distance pieces, the head, the tail, and the base — there should be seven pieces of ply in all. When you feel that all's correct, pencil press the lines of the design through to the working face of the ply. This done, go over the transferred lines with a 2B pencil, and clearly identify and label all the pieces.

Now put the wood in the vice, or clamp it to the workbench. Take the

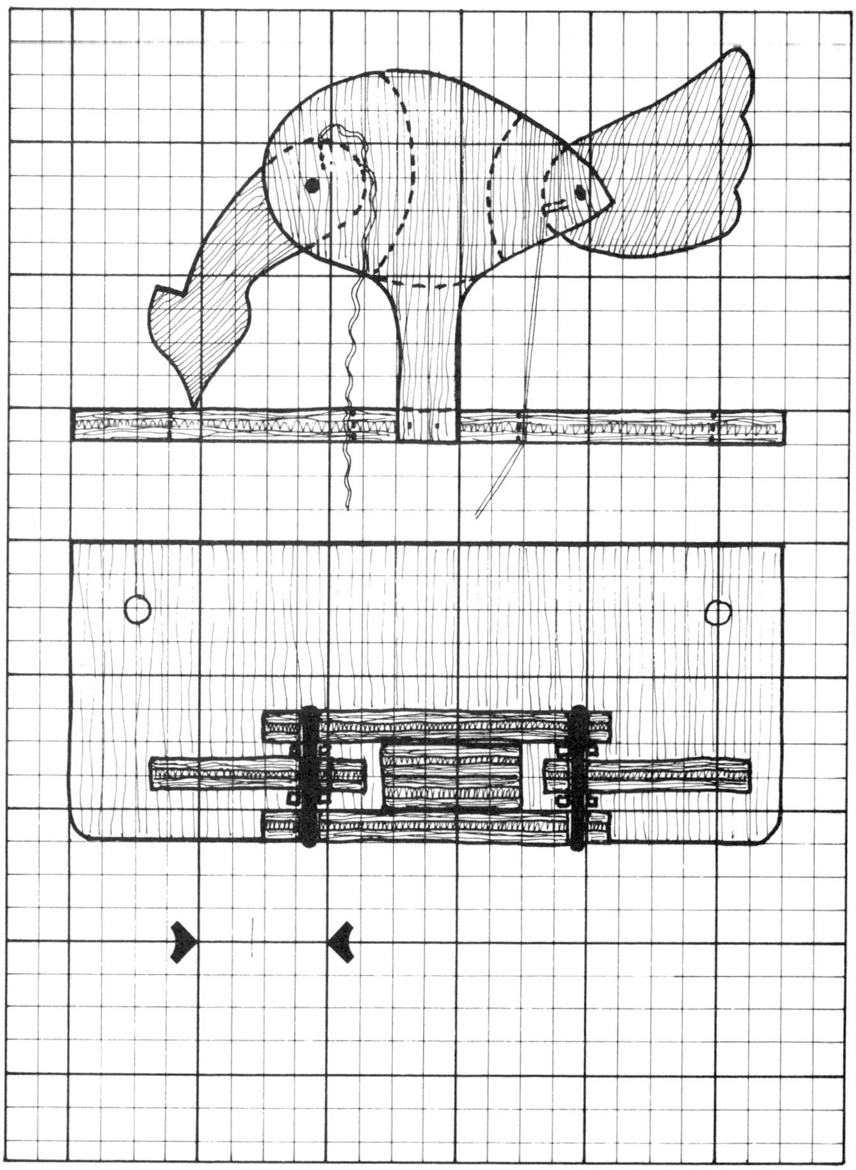

*Working Drawing, assembly grid – note the scale of four squares to one inch. The body of the chick has a total thickness of one inch, and the ¼ inch head and tail thickness needs to be packed out with washers.*

*When you come to cutting the enclosed slots, unclip one end of the coping saw blade, pass it through the pre-drilled hole, then re-assemble the saw and start sawing.*

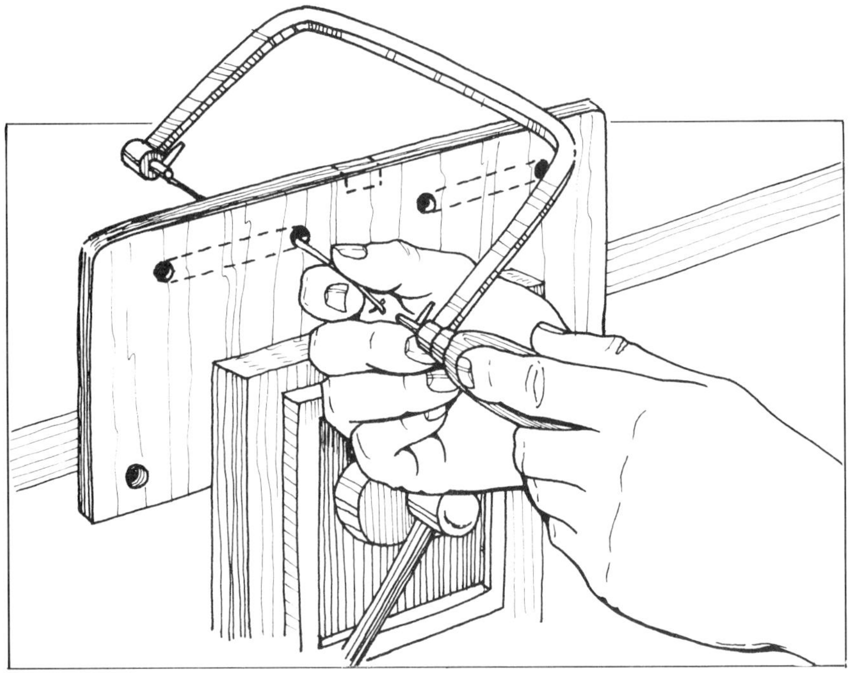

coping saw, making sure that the blade is well tensioned, then set about fretting out the drawn shapes. It's well worth mentioning at this stage, that the teeth of the coping saw blade can be pointing towards the handle, so that you cut on the backstroke, or pointing away from the handle, so that you cut on the downstroke; our advice is try both ways of working, and then go for the one that seems to suit you. So . . . back to work. Cut the wood with a considered gentle sawing action, don't rush, just try all the time to keep the cut edges crisp and at right angles to the working face of the wood.

Note – if, like us, you get carried away on a tide of anxious impatience, and just can't wait to see the toy finished, you will certainly break a blade or two. Don't be caught out and find yourself with a heap of broken blades and closed shops – always have a packet of spare blades.

## DRILLING THE PIVOTAL HOLES AND CUTTING THE MORTISES

Set your drill up with the 1/4 inch bit, have your knife and chisel at the ready, then put the wood to be worked in the vice. First drill the six pivotal holes, that is the holes in both chick body side plates, and the holes at the neck and tail. Now, this done, set the base-board in the vice, and establish the position of the various cuts – pay particular attention to the two screw holes, the two pendulum string slots, and the two mortise holes.

When you are sure that the base-plate is correctly marked out, then to work! Drill two screw holes – a hole at each end of the two string slots, and a single pilot hole within the central mortise, as illustrated. Now set the wood in the vice, dismantle the coping saw, pass the blade through one of the drilled holes, then assemble the saw and cut out the enclosed shape. Bear in mind that as you work, so you will have to adjust the angle of the saw blade and also manoeuvre the wood in the vice. And so you continue, cutting out the two pendulum slots and the central mortise. This done, take the saw and cut the half-mortise at the edge of the bracket. Now, when all the enclosed holes have been sawn, take your chisel and knife, and square up the cut edges of wood. Finally, take a scrap of sandpaper and a flat stick-tool, and take all the wood to a good smooth finish.

## PLACING, GLUING AND LAMINATING

Set out the pieces of cut and worked ply, and then be ready with the hammer, PVA glue and the brass pins. First take up the two main body panels and the two distance pieces, and put them together so that you have a total wood thickness of 1 inch — see gridded section drawing.

Now check with our working drawing, then, when you are sure all's correct, glue, place and pin. This done, take up the glued and pinned chick's body and set its feet in the base mortises. As sure as God made little chicks, the holes will be too small, so be prepared to fiddle around and trim back for a perfect fit. However when you reckon that the legs are at right angles to the base plate, then glue and pin, as illustrated.

## RUBBING DOWN AND PAINTING

You should now have three main toy pieces in all, that is, the glued up body-to-stand, the head and the tail. Now it might be as well before you go any further, to have a trial dry run assemble. Note how the head and tail are pivoted within the chick's body, and how the string holes and washers fit in relationship to the hardwood pivot pins. Dismantle the toy and rub down the wood with graded sandpapers until it's absolutely smooth to the touch.

Now wipe down your worksurface and set out the various paints and brushes. Bear in mind, before you start painting, that it's a lengthy business —

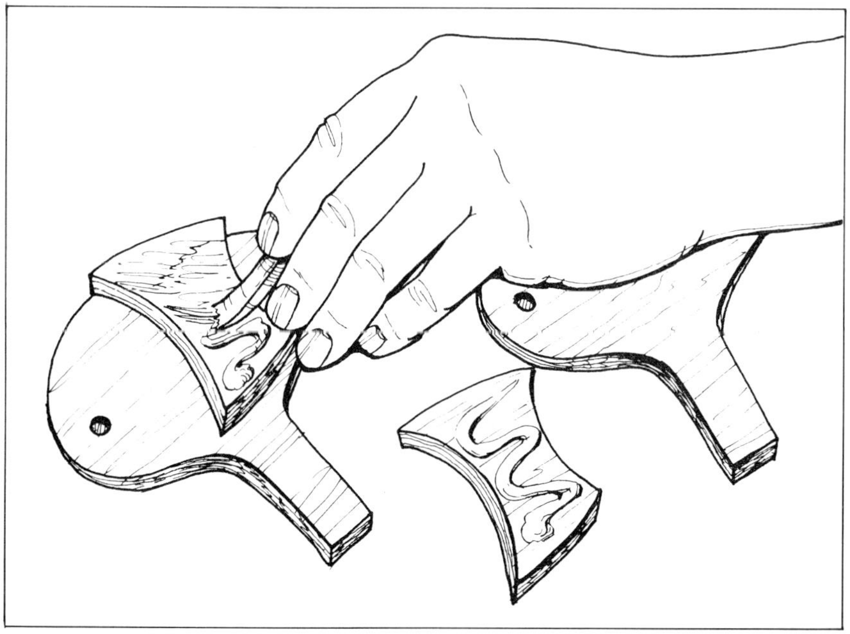

*Dab a little glue on the body spacers, then carefully place the laminated body in a clamp.*

*When the PVA glue is dry, fit and pin the body into the base mortises.*

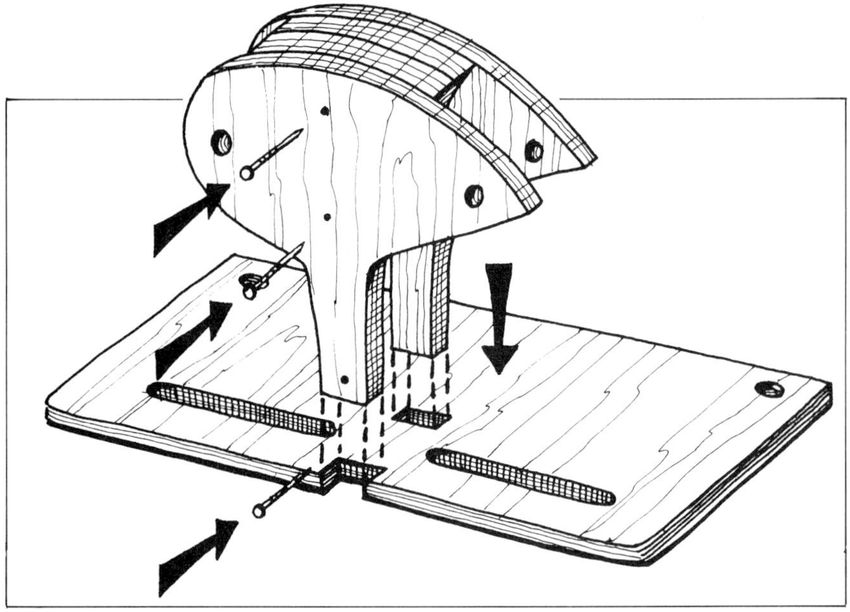

a primer, an undercoat, a topcoat, a final detail multi-colour coat, and of course the paint between coats needs to dry and be rubbed down. The whole painting stage might take four or five days – our advice is to set aside a special area for painting, then you won't have to worry about wood dust and the need to pack-away. Okay, so now you are organized and the wood to be painted is supported, as shown in previous projects.

Lay on a primer, an undercoat, a ground gloss topcoat, and finally, when the topcoat is completely dry, take a fine brush and good strong colours, and pick out and line-in the pattern and motif details of the feathers, eyes, tail and legs.

*When the chick/base, the head and tail have been painted, take a small knife and clean out the various pivotal holes.*

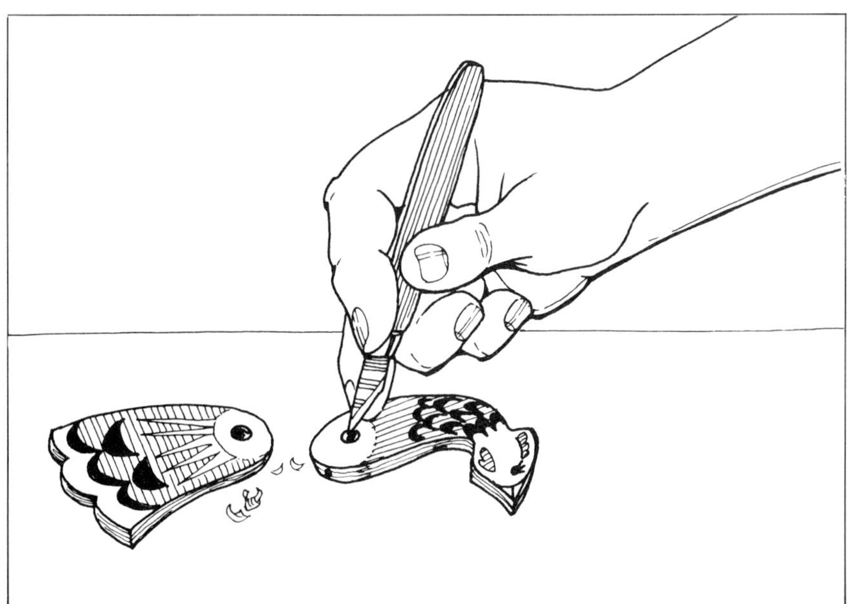

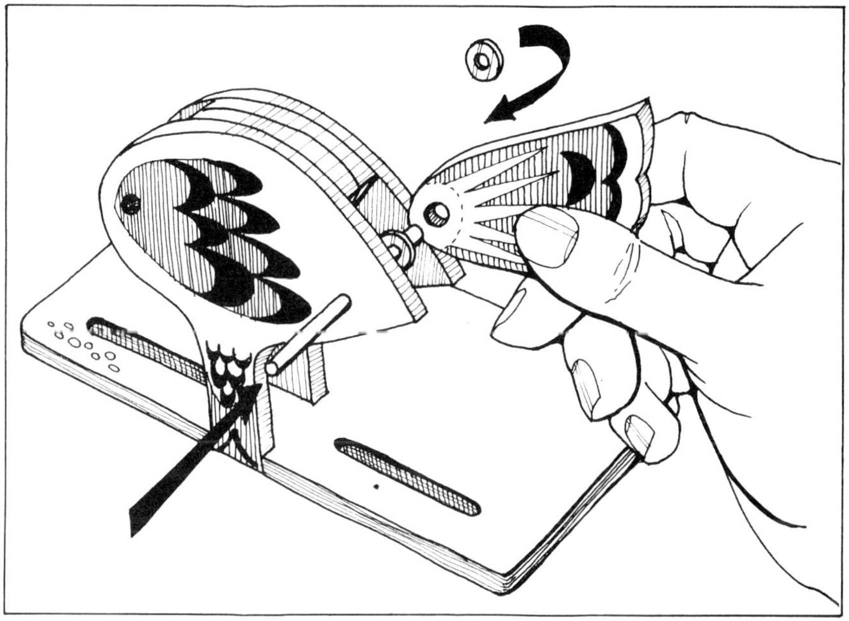

*Place the tail in the body cavity, position the washers, then push home the dowel. Do this for the head also.*

## BRINGING TOGETHER THE PIVOT RODS AND PENDULUM

When the paint is dry, cut the ¼ inch dowel rods to size, clear out the head and tail pivot holes, making sure that they are a good loose fit, then assemble the toy, as illustrated. This done, trim off the ends of the dowel rods and fix them with a few dabs of PVA glue. The chick's head and tail should now

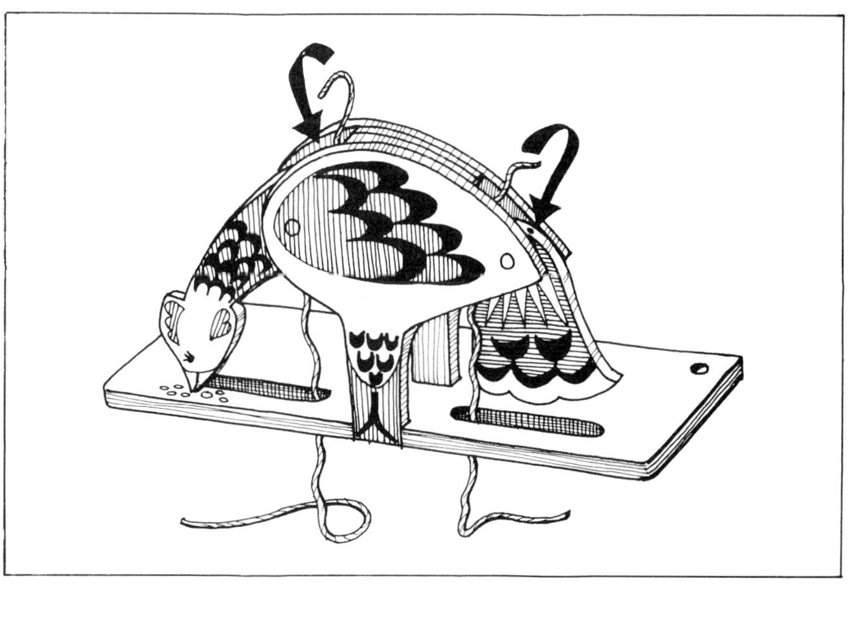

*When the pivotal rods are in place, let the head and tail flop down so that the two edge holes are in view, then glue, place, and peg the ends of the pendulum strings.*

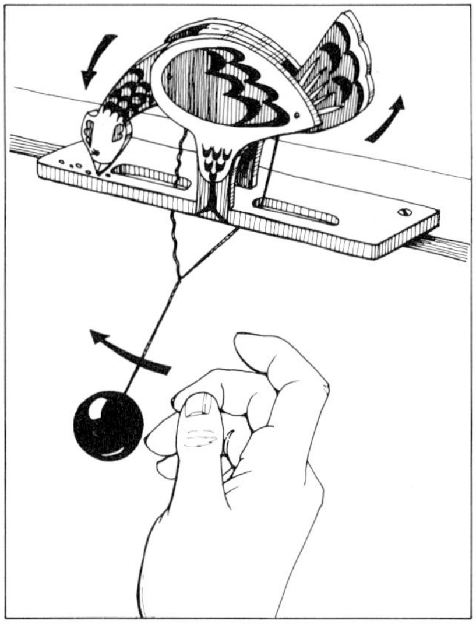

*In use, the pendulum is swung backwards and forwards so that the weight shifts from head to tail. In this drawing, for the sake of clarity, we have reduced the length of the pendulum strings – you will have to, by trial and error, adjust the string lengths and weight to suit your toy.*

swing freely on the dowel rods. Now take the ends of the pendulum cord, and glue, poke, push, plug and fix it into the tail and head holes.

Finally, add your chosen pendulum bob weight, screw or clamp the chick to a shelf or table top, and set the pendulum in motion. If all's well, when the pendulum is swung, the chick's head and tail will bob up and down – a beautiful toy!

## AFTERTHOUGHTS

If you have problems fixing the pendulum cord into the edge-wood of the tail and head, you might prefer to drill the wood through its ¼ inch thickness and tie and knot the cord.

It is most important that the pendulum bob be nicely weighted so that it counterbalances the chick's head and tail; we chose to use a bob made up of beads because it's possible to adjust the weight, little by little, just by adding beads.

When you have painted the head and tail, and the paint is dry, scrape out the pivotal holes and make sure that they are a very loose fit of about ⅜ inch.

If you are making this toy for a pre-school child, and see it as being a sort of over-cot or nursery mobile, then you must either make sure that the child can't reach it, or you must modify the design so that the cord has a very low breaking point – beads and cord loops aren't a good idea when children are at the put-it-in-the-mouth-and-suck stage.

PROJECT FIVE

# JUMPING JACK CLOWN

TOY TYPE · PIVOTAL LIMBS, AND STRINGS

## THOUGHTS ON THE PROJECT

Looking at a great many of our modern plastic cloned toys, it's hard to believe that there was a time, not so long ago, when if a child wanted a plaything, usually the parents or grandparents actually set-to and made one. Not for yesterday's children a whole heap of mass produced so called 'educational' toys — they had beautifully worked and painted wooden farmyard animals, pull-along and wheeled hobbyhorses, jointed take-to-bed dolls, and all manner of wonderfully imaginative home built toys. Now our parents, grandparents and great grandparents weren't especially gifted, nor were they able to spend vast sums of money buying in materials; no they used basic tools and 'found' scraps of wire, card, wood and string. These DIY amateur toymakers of course didn't just pluck ideas out of the air, they remembered their own favourite toys, and no doubt also unconsciously drew inspiration from European folk toys or fairings that could be seen at the saint's day fairs.

The best toys of this pre-plastic age were made of wood — sturdy uncomplicated toys that let children use their imagination, toys that to heighten the child's delight, moved, jerked or jumped. One such toy is the Jumping Jack who in his many forms and guises — monkeys, clowns and pirates, to name but a few, jerked and flapped his string operated limbs. Eighteenth century French children know Jumping Jack as 'pantin', that is to say cardboard cut-out Harlequin and Columbine figures — in West Germany he was known as Hampelmann and in the Thuringian forest he was called Zappelman, and so we could go on. Toys of the Jumping Jack type have, at some time or other, been made in places as far apart in time and space as ancient Egypt, nineteenth century Maori New Zealand, Japan, China and Central America. Of course all these folk, tribal and ethnic Jumping Jacks were related to local myths, stories and materials, and made of everything from wood to pottery, but they all had the same mechanical characteristics — that is, when a string, ring or hook is pulled, the limbs jerk and swing.

We've chosen to design and make a Jumping Jack with a modern clown image, and we've also modified the mechanism so that he doubles up as a wall-mounted peg or hook. The basic idea was inspired by a Jumping Jack Parrot that is currently being imported from India, and a Russian made, museum piece owl.

*Inspirational — a nineteenth century, Russian wood carved and painted owl jumping-jack type wallhook — put a weight on the hook, and the arms/wings flip up.*

## MATERIALS

For this project you need a piece of white faced ¼ inch thick multiply that measures about 9×9 inches, two small brass ³/₈ inch long screws, a shop-bought screw, hook, or picture-ring to hang the clown on the wall, a white PVA wood glue, a selection of model makers enamel paints, a white wood primer, a suitable undercoat, and about 12 inches of nylon cord.

**Tools** You need a bench vice or work-table clamp, a coping saw, a hand drill with a ¹/₈ inch drill bit, a pack of graded sandpapers, a selection of small shaped stick-tools (see 'Tools and Materials' section), a small screwdriver, a pair of scissors, fine and large brushes, and last, but not least, pencils, workout paper and tracing paper.

*Working Drawing painting grid – note the scale of four squares to one inch. We've given our clown a modern, almost cartoon image, but there's no reason why you shouldn't go for a period motif.*

## CONSIDERING THE PROJECT

Before you start, have a look at our working drawings and step-by-step details, and see how the Jumping Jack mechanism operates — that is to say, how the arms swing up when the boot-shaped hook is pulled down. You might also consider at this stage whether or not you want to copy our design direct, or maybe work a Jumping Jack that has a strong period feel, say a Harlequin or even a figure inspired by a modern popular personality. When you understand just how the toy operates, it might be as well to visit local

*Working Drawing, assembly grid – note the scale of four squares to one inch. See how by pulling down on the hook the arms flip up. Note – the arms have to hang heavy, otherwise they won't fall down when the hook weight is removed.*

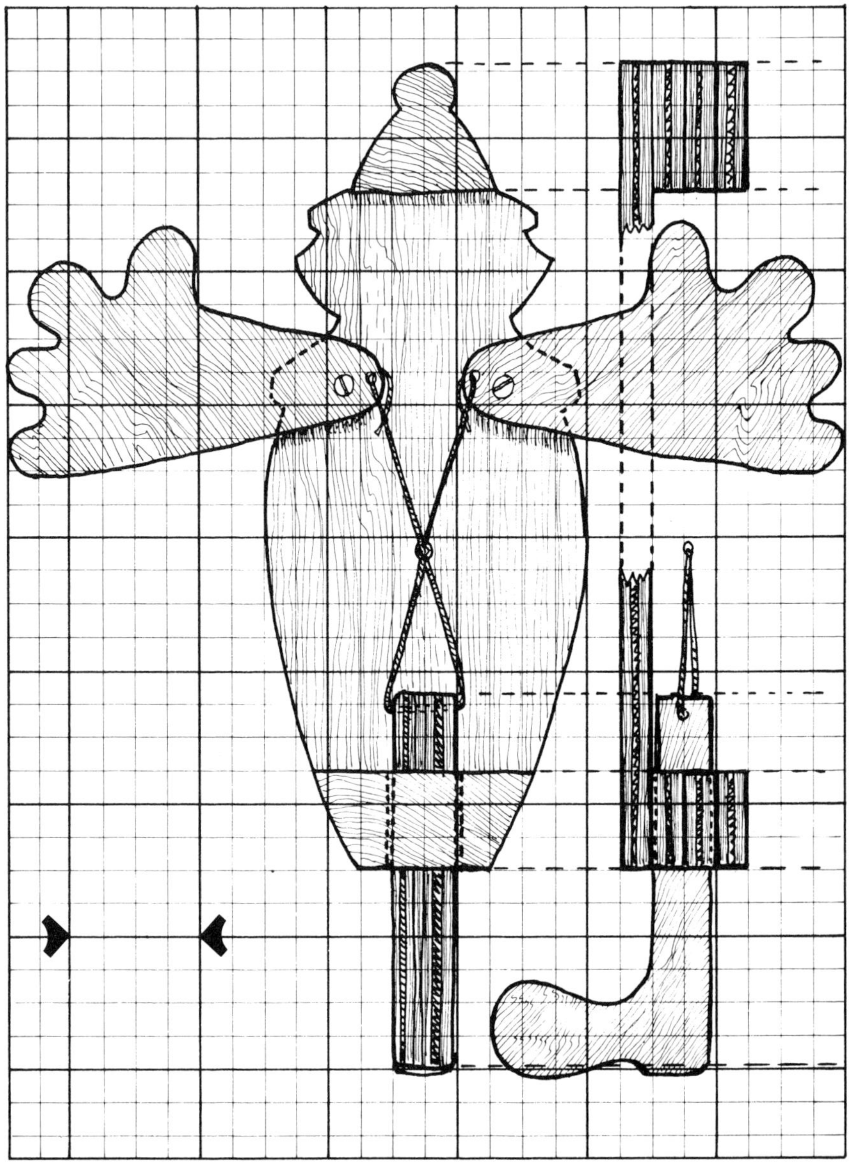

craft and toy museums and see if you can search out some exciting inspirational material.

Finally, look through old magazines – you might just come up with some interesting pictures and photographs, for example, clowns in costume and make-up.

*Working Drawing, cutting grid – note the scale of four squares to one inch – there are thirteen toy components in all.*

## SETTING OUT THE DESIGN AND CUTTING THE MULTIPLY

Have a look at the working drawing grids, and see how the clown is built up, sandwich-like, out of layers of ¼ inch ply. Draw out your designs, checking that any modifications don't upset the hook and string mechanism, then, using a soft pencil and tracing paper, transfer the lines of the design to the working face of the wood. Your sheet of ply should now be set out with

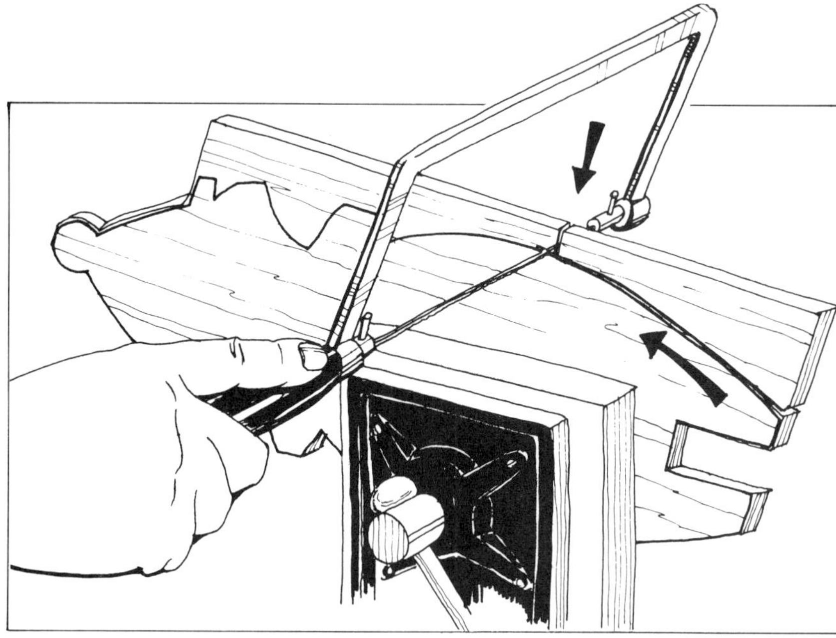

*Transfer the design to the working face of the wood, put the wood in the vice, and then set-to with the coping saw.*

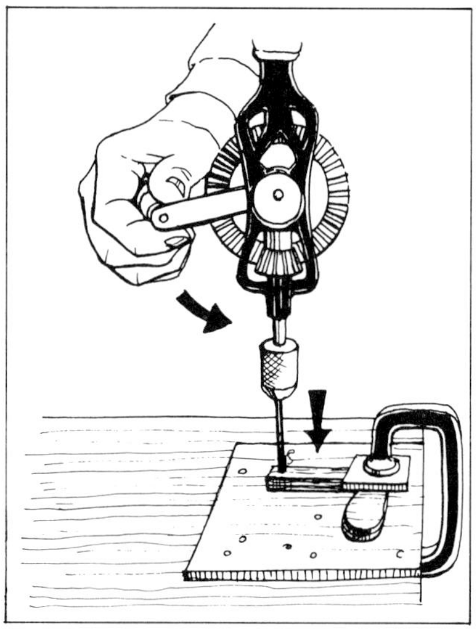

*When you have cut out all the parts and established the position of the various pivotal holes, clear them with a hand drill. See how we have used a clamp and backing board, and how the drill is held at right angles to the working face of the wood.*

thirteen shapes in all, the main clown body, two arms, three little hats, two boot shaped hooks, four shapes that go to make up the channel or hook guide, and a hook guide backing plate.

When you've checked that all is correct, and you're confident that your design modifications are going to work, pencil label all the drawn out elements, 'body', 'hook 1', 'hook 2' and so on. This done, clamp your wood in the vice and set-to with the coping saw. Work at a steady pace, trying all the

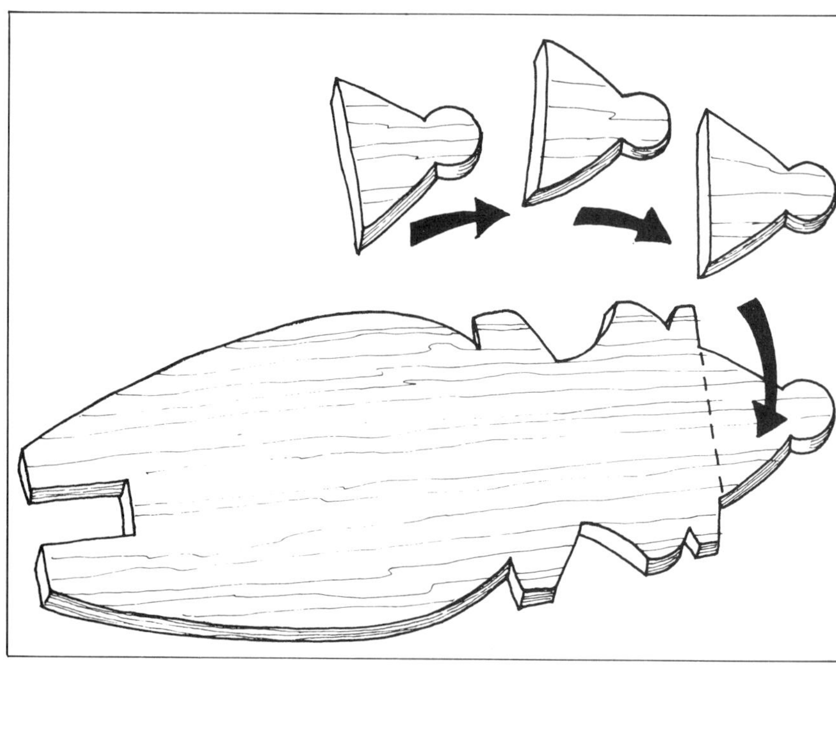

*Take the three little hat cut-outs, use a spot or two of PVA glue and build up the total hat thickness of 1 inch.*

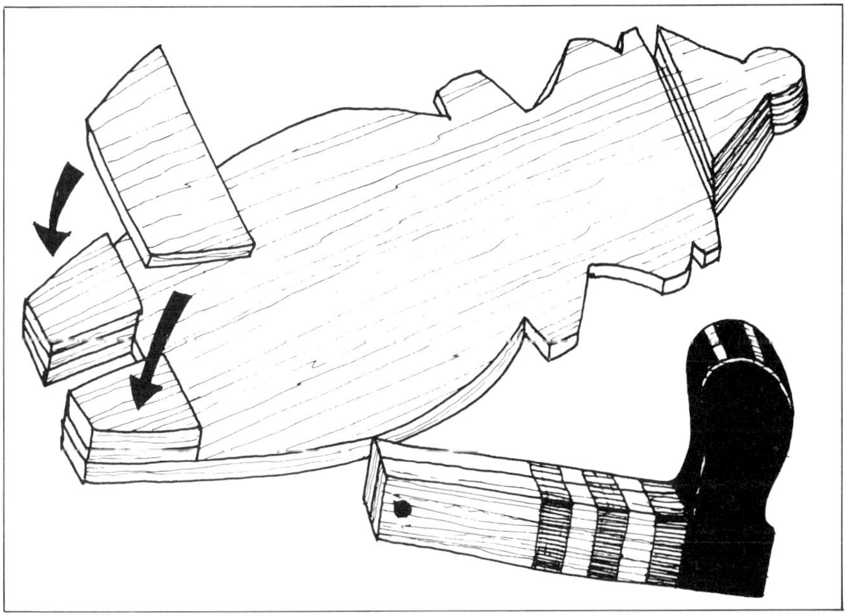

*Use PVA glue to build up the guide channel layers, wait for the glue to set, then rub down and paint.*

while to keep the saw blade at right-angles to the working face of the wood. When you saw, don't twist the blade, or be in a rush to finish, but rather keep the cut to the outside of the drawn lines of the design – keep the blade moving, even when you're cutting sharp angle corners, and aim for cuts that are crisp and clean.

## GLUING AND LAMINATING

When you have cut out the various pieces, take the graded sandpapers and the shaped stick tools, and rub off all the sharp burrs, edges and angles. This done, take the white PVA glue, and start to build-up the various laminations – that is to say, the layers that go to make up the clowns hat, the leg hook, the guide channel and the back plate. Don't go wild with the glue, just give the various ply layers a thin smear, then carefully bring them together in the correct order. Finally, press the glued wood between clamped boards, or pop it in the vice for twenty-four hours.

## DRILLING, RUBBING DOWN, PRIMING AND PAINTING

When the glue is dry, take the drill and the $^1/_8$ inch bit, and work the five holes, a pivotal hole in each arm, and three string holes – one at the top of the hook shaft, and one in each arm – see working drawing details.

Now take the sandpaper, and rub down all the glued and drilled components until they are completely smooth edged and free from burrs. You should now have four toy parts in all, two arms, a single ½ inch thick boot-shaped hook, and of course the main clown form with its glued and laminated additions.

Before you take the toy any further, consider how the glued laminations fit together to add up to a total wood thickness of 1 inch, and see how the boot/hook shaft slides in its channel. Now, bearing in mind that you will be painting the wood, and so building up the total thickness, take the sandpaper and further rub down the hook shaft until it's a very loose fit. Once you have rubbed down all the corners, angles and edges, wipe down the worksurface with a damp cloth and remove all the dust, then be ready with the white primer, the undercoat, the gloss enamel, and the various brushes, cleaners and cloths.

Now for a quality finish, lay on a white primer, one or two undercoats and the gloss topcoat. Don't ladle the paint on, but rather lay it on in very thin coats, and when each coat is dry and needs rubbing down, make sure that you do it well outside the painting area.

Finally when the top ground colour/colours are dry, and you have established the main design motifs, say the hair, face, arms and trousers, then take the fine brush and pick out the design details. Don't try to work subtle colour blends, much better to go for hard edged, bold, graphic primary colours, and then to pick out the details with crisp strokes, lines, dabs and dashes of red, gold, white and black.

## ASSEMBLY AND BRINGING TOGETHER

Take the four Jumping Jack parts, all worked, rubbed down, drilled and painted, as described and illustrated, set them down on a clean worksurface, and have at hand the cord, scissors, measure, two small brass screws and the screwdriver. Lay the main clown form face down, establish the exact position of the two pivot points, then fix the arms to the clown body with the screws. Bear in mind that you only have a total wood thickness of ½ inch, so be careful that you don't overwork the screws and splinter or split the wood.

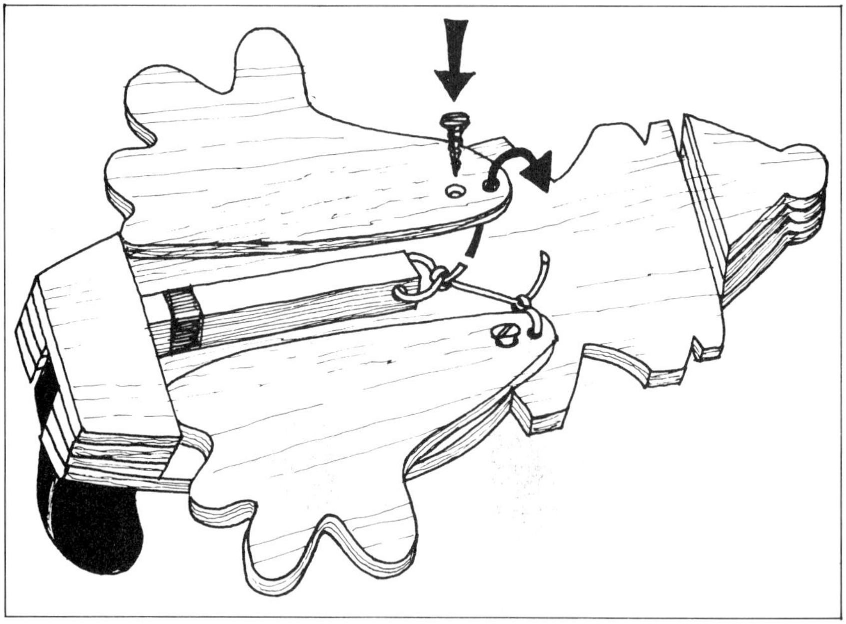

*When all the clown components have been painted, wait for twenty-four hours for the paint to dry, then with screws and string put the little man together. Note – when the boot is in the 'up' position, the hands should be in the 'down'.*

Now with the clown still face down, but supported on a couple of blocks, pass the boot shaft up through the guide channel. This done, place the arms at the 'at rest' position, then tie and knot the cord link-up; the cord is knotted at one arm hole, it then goes down through the hook-shaft hole, then back up to the other arm hole.

Now for the big test – hold the Jumping Jack, right-side-up, against a wall and gently pull down on the hooked boot. If the hook slides down and the

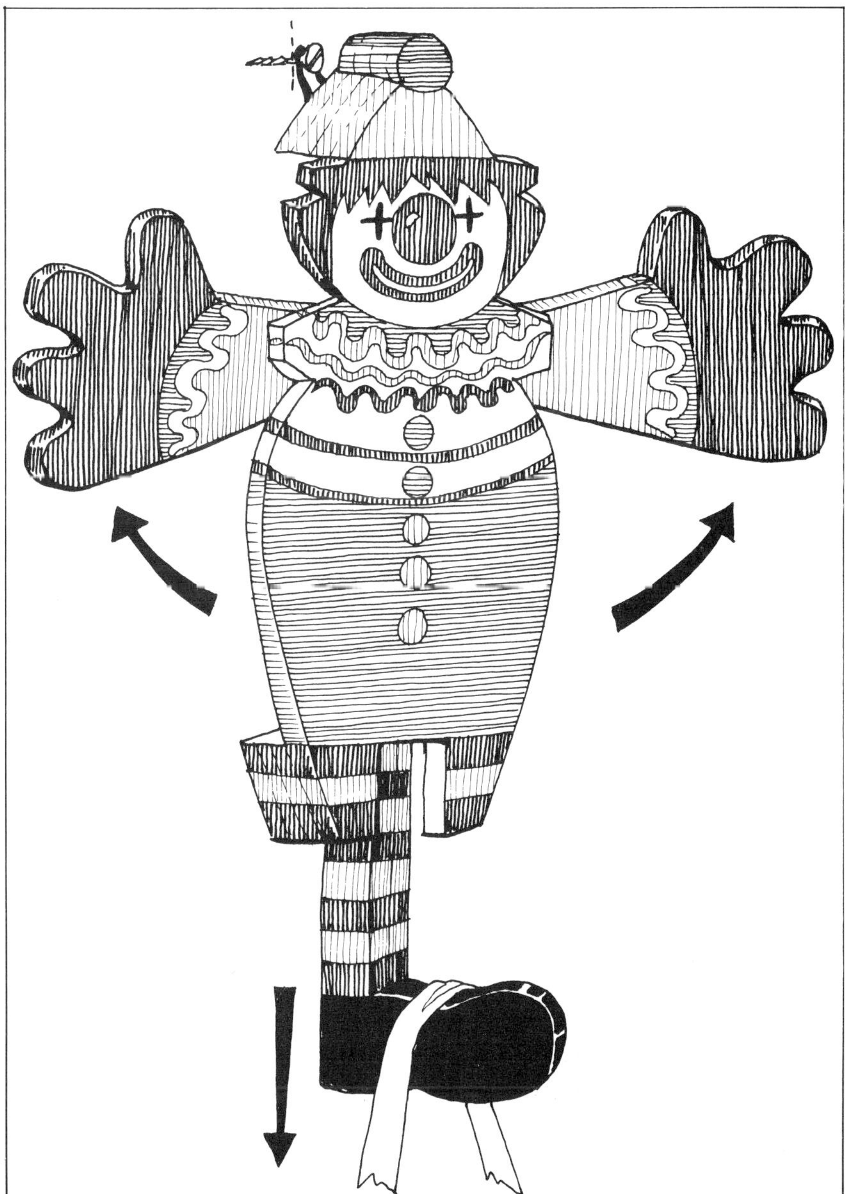

*In use, the clown is wall mounted and then used for a lightweight clothes hook – say for a hat or some such.*

arms flip up, then you're onto a winner! Finally, screw mount the Jumping Jack to say a child's bedroom door or whatever, and invite the child to hang up his/her dressing gown. A toy, and a jolly way of encouraging the child to keep his bedroom tidy — what more could you ask for?

## AFTERTHOUGHTS

This particular Jumping Jack is about nine inches from tip to toe, and only designed to take say the weight of a towel or a small item of dress, but there is no reason at all why you shouldn't double up all the measurements, use ½ inch multiply, and make a larger, stronger more complex toy with perhaps the arms and legs jointed at the wrists, elbows, knees and ankles.

With a bit of thought and modification at the design stage, maybe you could work a toy with an eye 'opening-and-closing' mechanism — it's a thought!

When you come to buying your wood, choose dense, white faced, multi-layer ply, and always reject wood that looks to be stained with rust, oil or grease.

It's most important, when you are painting, that the work area is dust free.

The guide channel and hook shaft need to be worked so that they are loose fitting; it might be an idea, at the initial cutting stage, to go for a narrower shaft.

If the arms swing up, but fail to fall down, screw counterweights to the back of the hands.

PROJECT SIX

# JOLLY JOHN THE GYMNAST

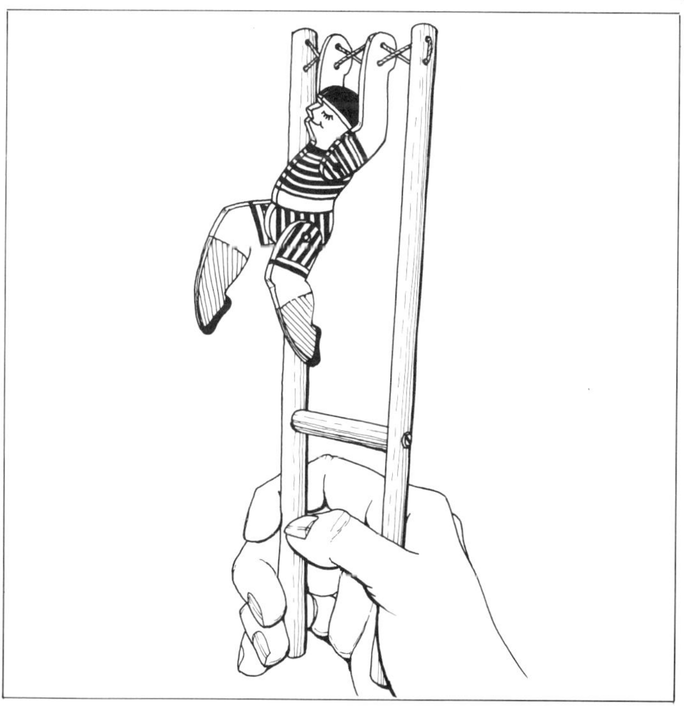

TOY TYPE · TWIST STRING AND PIVOTAL

## THOUGHTS ON THE PROJECT

The gymnast, acrobat or 'mechanical' swinging man, has been a favourite toy for well over two hundred years. We've seen country-rustic wind driven Whirligig acrobats that were made in Colonial America, pretty little wood carved 'bobbin' acrobats that were made in eighteenth century Austria and in Japan a hundred or so years ago, toymakers carved delicate ivory gymnasts. And so we could go on describing gymnast and acrobat toys that were made

*Working Drawing, painting grid – note the scale of four squares to one inch.*

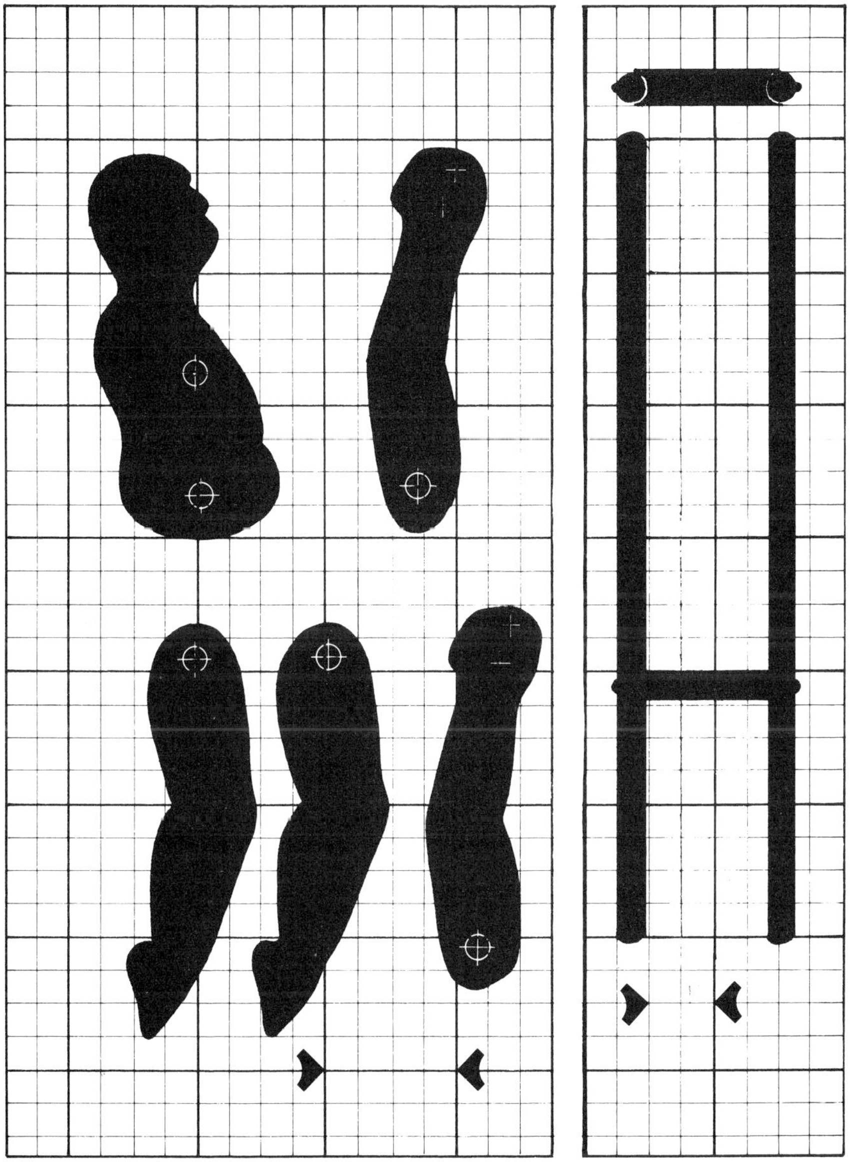

*Working Drawing, cutting grid – note that there are two scales: four squares to one inch for the man, and two squares to one inch for the two-stick frame.*

in such far away places as The Black Forest, Bavaria, Switzerland, Italy, Poland, France, Sweden and Russia.

However, of these toys, my favourite is a little two-stick gymnast that was probably made in England about 1890–1910; he's wood carved, painted so as to look like a Victorian circus acrobat or music hall gymnast, and he's operated by a simple twist-string mechanism. Hold the toy by the two sticks, clench them together so that the twisted string tightens, and upsy-daisy! the little man rises, swings over, and then does an amazing topsy-turvy star turn.

Toys of this classic character take a bit of beating; they're beautifully folk made out of basic materials, and their movement is ingenious and yet simple. Now don't think that these toys only belong to some obscure glorious long-gone tradition — not a bit of it. The other day, bemoaning our lot and grizzling on about nasty plastic toys, we looked in a shop window, and what do you think we saw? Well, you've guessed it — not one, not two, but a couple of bunches of modern gymnast toys. We could hardly believe our eyes, but there they were, charming little cut-ply figures, all stencil decorated with what looked to be a Tyrolean policeman type outfit, and better still they

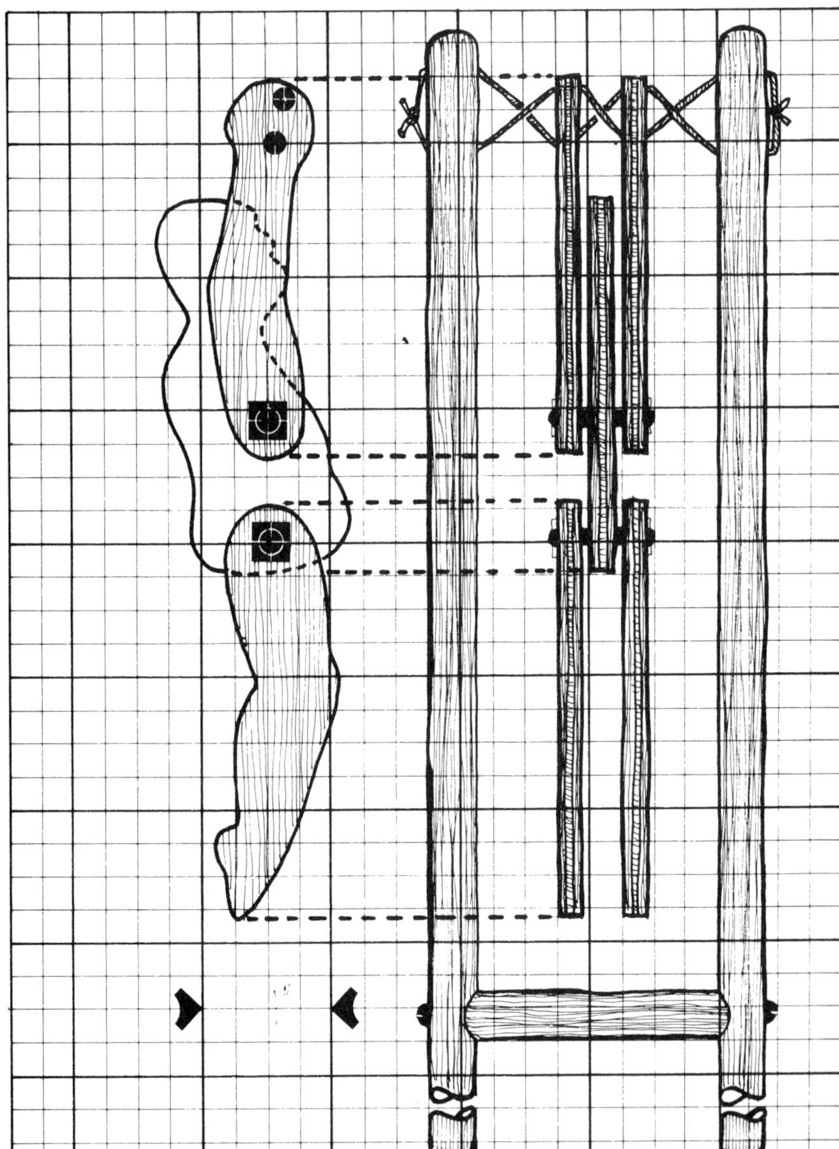

*Working Drawing, assembly grid – note the scale of four squares to one inch. See how the riveted limbs are a loose fit, and how the frame crossbar is screwed.*

were selling at only 35p each. Hurrah! the centuries old tradition of cheap, folk-made 'penny' and 'fairing' toys is alive and well.

## CONSIDERING THE PROJECT

Sit back with a pencil and sketch paper, have a long slow look at our working drawings, and see how the toy is made up from $^3/_{16}$ inch multiply and $^3/_8$ inch diameter dowel. Take note of the loose-jointed body, the double-twisted loop-string mechanism, and the screw fixed dowel cross-bar. Now run your eyes over the various grid scales and consider the stick measurement of 12 inches, and the gymnast, finger-to-toes, measurement of about 6 inches.

Now, at this stage, as with all the projects, you can if you so wish, adjust and modify the design to suit your own needs, For example, you can have square section wood instead of dowel, you can have cord pivots or screws instead of soft copper rivets, you can change the figure's costume, and so on. The only thing we would advise against is making the gymnast larger; the size and weight of the figure, sticks and string, are all critical.

Finally, when you have studied all the working drawings and you understand just how the string mechanism works, look through magazines, books on costume, illustrated Victoriana and the like, then take your workout paper and felt tips, and see if you can rework and improve upon our inspirational designs and motifs.

## MATERIALS

For this project you need a piece of white faced, $^3/_{16}$ inch multiply that measures about 6×6 inches, 28 inches of $^3/_8$ inch dowel; two $^1/_8$ inch

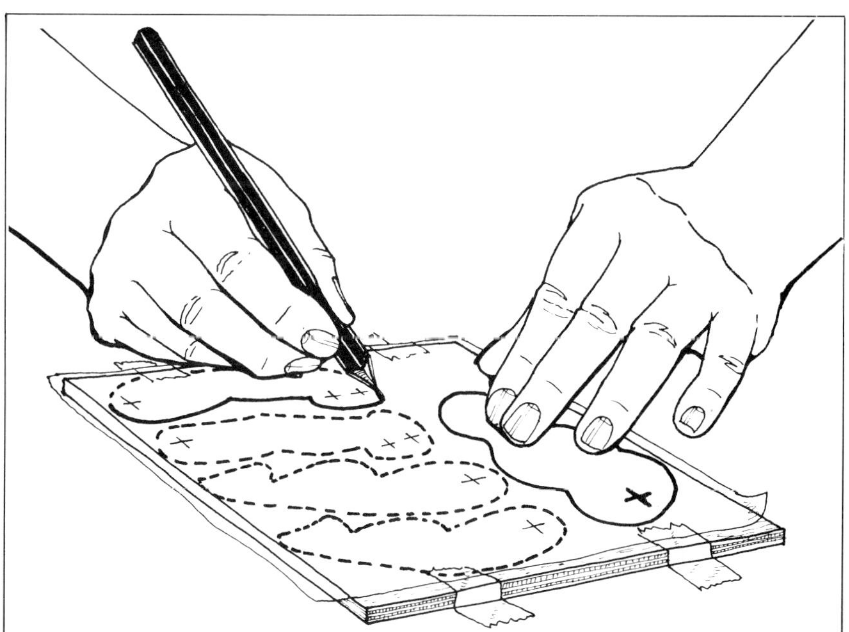

*Use tracing paper, and pencil press transfer the lines of the design onto the surface of the wood. See how the wood and the tracing paper are held with sticky-tape tags.*

diameter, 1 inch long copper/brass white metal rivets, four brass washers to fit the rivets, two slender 1 inch brass dome-head screws, about 12 inches of strong fine cotton or linen cord, and, last but not least, you need a selection of model makers paints, a primer and an undercoat.

**Tools** You need the use of a bench vice or worktable holdfast, a fine-blade coping saw or fret saw, a hand drill with a $1/8$ inch drill bit, a light ball-end hammer, an iron block (see project), a pair of pliers, a model makers file, a pack of graded sandpapers, a small screwdriver, a sharp knife, a pencil and ruler, tracing paper, and finally a couple of soft hair brushes, cloths and a cleaner.

## SETTING OUT THE DESIGN

Take your workout paper, a pencil and a ruler, and draw out the five gymnast parts – that is the head/body torso, the two arms, and the two legs. Now check the overall measurements, and then, when you're sure all's correct, trace the design, and pencil press transfer the lines of the design through to the working face of the wood. This done, re-work the transferred lines, establish the various pivotal and string holes, then label the shapes, 'arm', 'leg', etc.

## CUTTING AND DRILLING

When you are happy with the way the shapes are set out, clamp the wood in the vice and then set-to with your chosen saw. That is, you cut in from the ply edges, and then carefully turn the wood and manoeuvre the saw, until all five shapes have been nicely fretted out. Don't hurry or try to force the pace; just work steadily and try to keep the blade at 90° to the working face of the wood.

This done, clear away the scrap, brush down the worksurface, and be

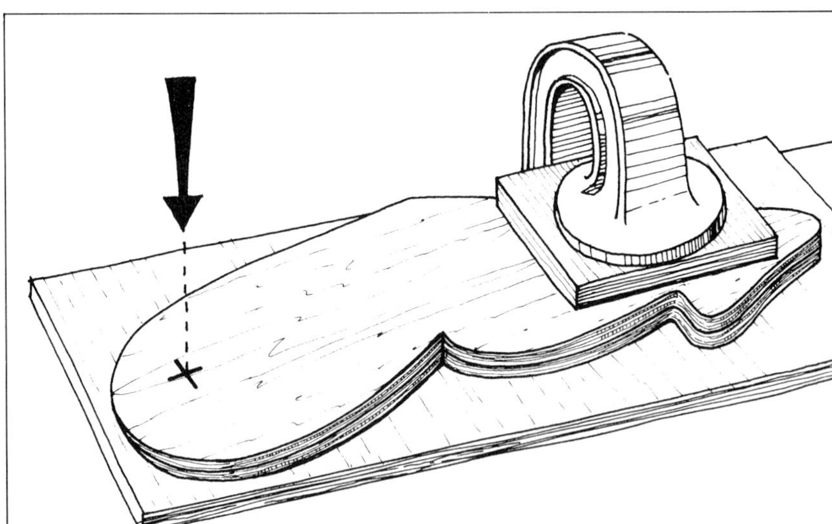

*The limbs are carefully clamped to the bench, the pivot points are established and the holes are drilled.*

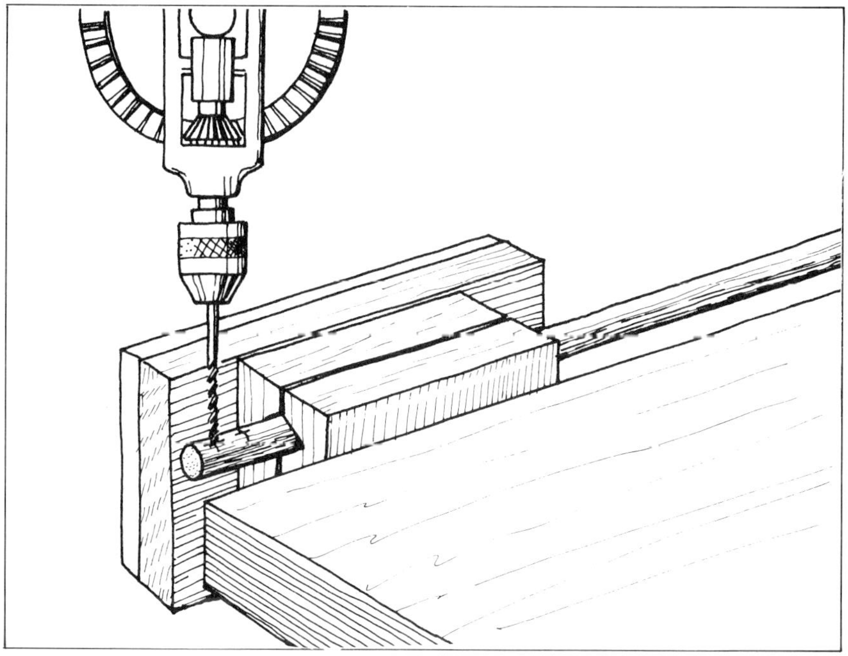

*When you come to drilling holes in the frame sticks, it might be an idea to secure the dowel, in a couple of easy-to-make vice clamps.*

ready with the hand drill and 1/8 inch drill bit. Place both of the gymnast's legs together, as illustrated, clearly mark the pivot point, then, using a scrap wood backing, drill and work the hole. Now repeat the procedure with the arms, but this time drill three holes — one for the pivot, and two for the twist-string mechanism. Finally, drill the two pivot holes in the body of the gymnast.

Now stop awhile, maybe have a cup of coffee, and carefully check with the working drawings that all the holes are well placed. When you are sure that all is as it should be, take a stick-tool and a scrap of sandpaper, and take all the pieces of wood to a good finish. That is to say, clean out the drilled holes and rub down all the contours, profiles and cut edges until they are perfectly smooth and round to the touch.

## PAINTING

Clear away all the wood dust and bench clutter, or better still move to a special dust-free painting area; then set out the paints, brushes, cleaner and the wood to be painted. Now don't rush head down into the painting, but rather organize some sort of support or drying frame, and generally establish in your mind's eye, or better still down on paper, just how you want the gymnast to be painted. This done, lay on a primer, an undercoat and a topcoat, as already described in other projects.

Finally, have another last good look at all your design sketches, then with a fine-point brush, and your chosen colours, pick out the various motifs, patterns and details.

*The painting area needs to be well set out, note the knotted line, the hooked wires and the cover paper.*

## MAKING THE 'H' FRAME

Take your 28 inches of dowel, and cut it down so that you have three pieces — two at 12 inches and one at 2 inches. Now take the two 12 inch dowels and round-up the cut ends with a knife and sandpaper. This done, take a measure,

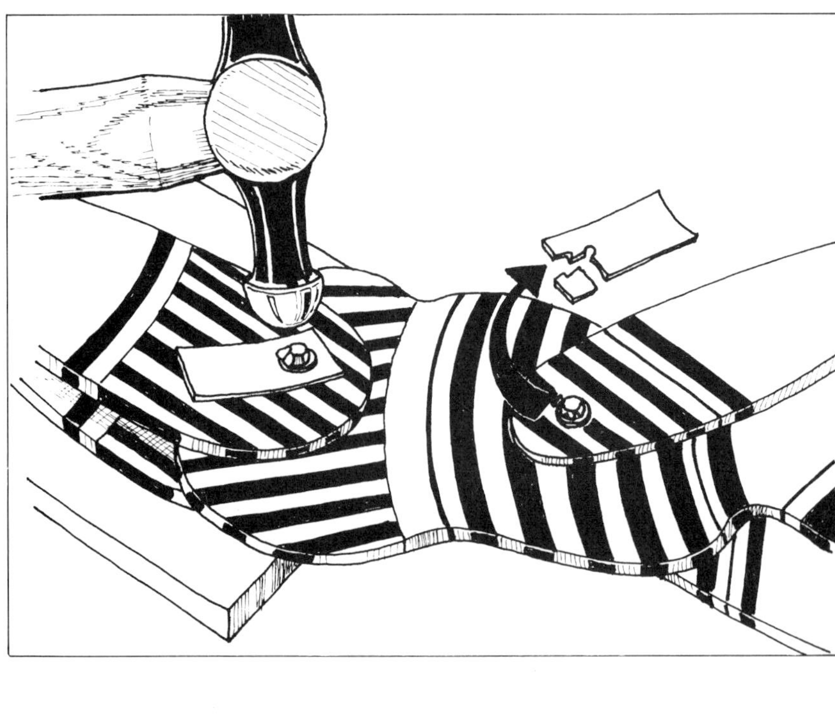

*Support the rivet, head down, on an iron plate, use a little card spacer and protector, then position the washer and tap down the tail of the rivet with a lightweight ball-pein hammer. See how that after the rivet has been 'mushroomed', the card protector is torn away.*

pencil and $^1/_8$ inch drill, and work the two 12 inch dowels, as illustrated — that is to say, so that each has a 'cross-bar' hole and two twist-string holes.

Now with a knife, sandpaper and a scrap of dowel, shape the ends of the little cross-bar dowel so that they are a concave snug fit. Finally, take the two small brass screws and fit the 'H' frame together as shown.

## RIVETING AND PUTTING TOGETHER

Set the little gymnast out in its correct order, then be ready with the copper rivets, the washers and the hammer. Working the rivets one at a time, hold the unit so that the rivet is supported, head-down, on an iron block or plate. Now take the round faced hammer, and tap-over the tail of the rivet with a dozen or so well placed glancing blows. Aim to spread the rivet so that its tail is rounded and nicely mushroomed against the washer, as illustrated. Finally, take the model makers file and work the taped-over rivets to a smooth burr-free finish.

This done, clear the worksurface of all the mess and scrap, spread out a piece of old sheeting (so that your toy doesn't get scratched), then set out the 'H' frame, the gymnast and the length of cord. Place the gymnast between the 'H' uprights, and position him so that his arms are outstretched. Now take the cord, and thread-and-link the dowels and the gymnast's hands. The cord, left to right, goes from the bottom dowel hole, up to the top 'hand' hole, down to the bottom 'hand' hole, up to the top dowel hole, down to a dowel hole, up to a 'hand' hole, down to a 'hand' hole, and finally up to the top dowel hole where it is knotted off. We know it all sounds incredibly finger twisting, but in fact it's very simple, as long as you bear in mind that the strings need to cross when they travel between holes.

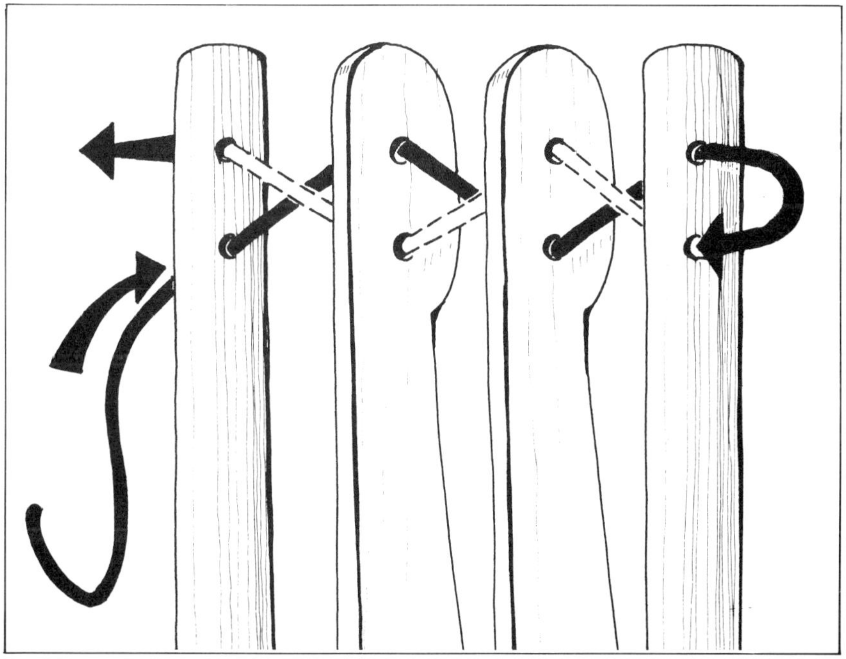

*The threading pattern for the twist-string mechanism.*

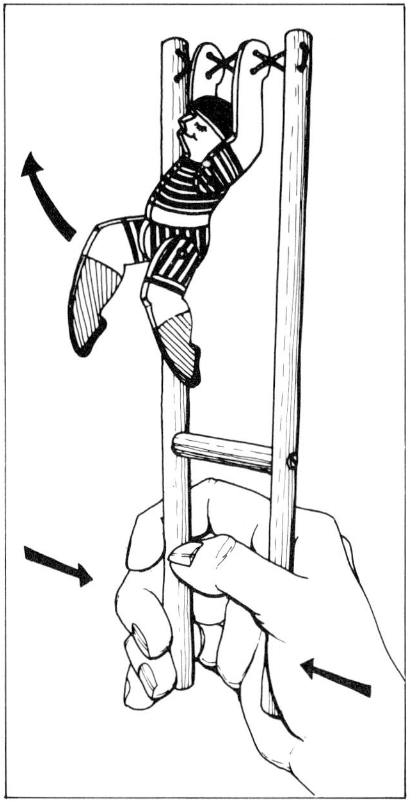

*In use, the two sticks are gently squeezed – the twisted string tightens and turns, and the man flips over.*

Now for the big test – hold the bottom prongs of the 'H' frame so that the gymnast hangs freely on slack strings, then gently squeeze the sticks together. If the top of the 'H' widens, the crossed strings tighten, and the gymnast swings up and over, then you're onto a winner.

## AFTERTHOUGHTS

The measurement of the gymnast, from toes to outstretched finger tips, must not exceed the top 'H' frame measurement of 8 inches (see working drawings). The gymnast needs to be loose limbed; you can use rivets, bolts or knotted cord, but on no account must you use limb-glued wooden rods.

If, like us, you blunder and drill a pivot hole in the wrong place, don't panic, just fill it with a resin/hardener filler and make good. Always give time and effort to the rubbing down; don't settle for anything less than a perfect finish. Note that the 28 inches of dowel allows for a couple of inches of wastage.

When you're tapping over the tails of the rivets, you need to support the rivet heads on an iron block – we use an old flat-iron, clamped handle-down in the vice.

PROJECT SEVEN

# GALLOPING HUSSAR

TOY TYPE · COUNTERBALANCE

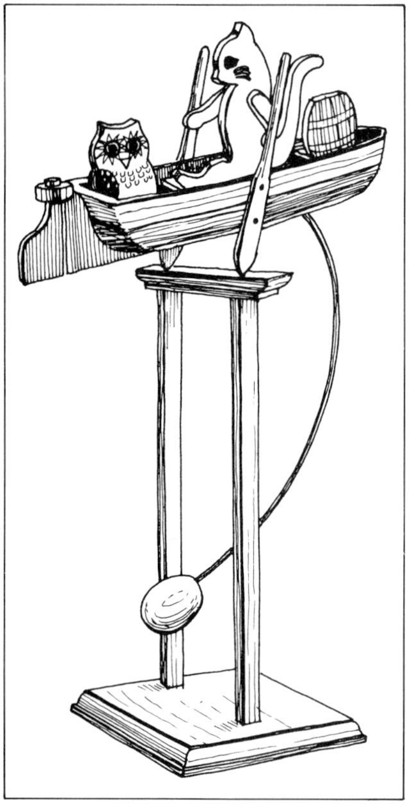

*Inspirational – an Edwardian 'home arts', owl and pussycat counterbalance toy.*

## THOUGHTS ON THE PROJECT

One of the joys of designing and making a wooden toy of this type, size and character, is the fact that you can re-shape the specifications, the working method, the materials, the techniques, and even the overall image to suit your own unique passions and inclinations. For example, if you are interested in the wonderful sculptural horse miniatures that were made by the pre-war Hampshire toymakers, you might choose to paint this toy with naturalistic colours, and really get involved in researching the hussar's uniform.

On the other hand, you might enjoy lathe work and want to re-think the design in terms of split spindle limbs, turned knobs and bobbin heads. And then again, you might want to relate the design image to say nineteenth century German folk toys, or maybe give it an American Colonial period feel. There are endless possible variations on the basic theme – our advice is to have a good look at the working drawings, see and understand how the toy operates, and then either copy the design direct, or adjust it to suit your own needs.

We decided, after a deal of consideration and museum research, to concentrate our efforts on making the horse and rider, and show him on a 'found' stand. When we initially designed the toy, we decided to pool and use the skills and talents of the whole family. I like working with flat graphic forms, my wife enjoys using bright colours and fine brushes, and our two teenage sons are interested in lathe-work – in no time at all this project lifted off and became a group effort.

Fortunately our mini, 'rural collective' approach is in keeping with the best toy making traditions, and certainly the end result has just the right naive and guileless feel. We have used good quality multiply for the horse and rider, and achieved a powerful Victorian image with model makers enamels and metallic paints.

## MATERIALS

For this project you need a 7×7 inch piece of white faced, good quality, ½ inch thick multiply, a length of coathanger wire, a white PVA wood glue, a small amount of resin glue, a selection of non-toxic model makers enamels, a suitable wood primer, two or three inches of ¼ inch hardwood dowel, a scrap of fine leather, small brass pins/screws, a coloured feather, a small swatch of coloured silk, and a turned ball/bead, or some-such, for the counterbalance bob.

**Tools** As for tools and equipment, you need a bench clamp or vice, a coping, fret, jig or band saw, a small hand drill with a ⅛ inch and ¼ inch drill bit, a pack of graded sandpapers, and of course such workshop items as pencils, brushes, measures, scrap paper, felt tips and tracing paper.

## WORKING AND TRANSFERRING THE MASTER DESIGN

Our Galloping Hussar, as illustrated, is worked to a 1 inch grid – see the horses nose-to-tail measurement of about 7 inches. Note – you can, if you so wish, adjust this project and use different motifs, say a dog, cat, camel, etc.

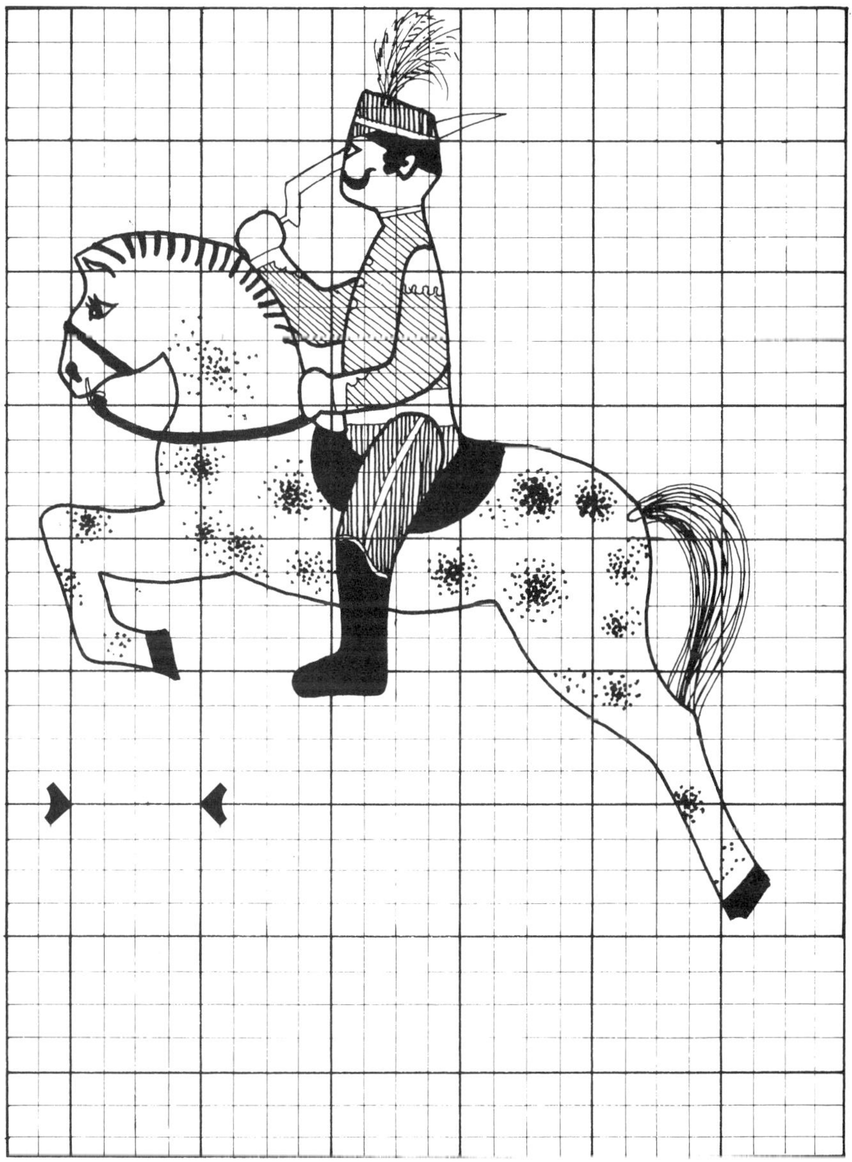

*Working Drawing, painting grid – note the scale of four squares to one ihch.*

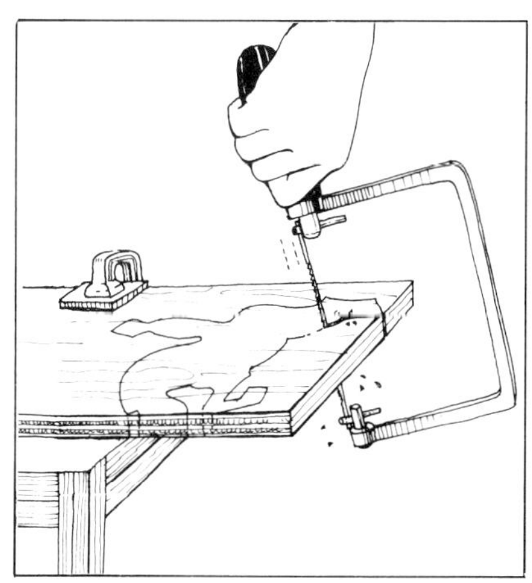

*Transfer the lines of the design to the working face of the wood, and then set-to with the coping saw.*

However if you do decide to adjust the design, it might be as well to knock up a scrap card and plasticine prototype, and check-out weight and counter-balance problems.

Consider all the design and material options, then, using a soft pencil and gridded paper, work out the main lines of the design. Now pencil press transfer the lines of the design to the working face of the piece of ½ inch thick ply (see working drawings). It's all relatively straightforward; you simply transfer and fit the five toy elements or bits; that is to say the horse/rider body and the four limbs, so that you make best and most economical use of the available material.

It's well worth sitting back at this stage and making sure that you haven't overdesigned the image or given it unworkable details: are the forms nicely rounded? are there any short grain areas that might cause problems? — these are all points to consider before you actually put tool to wood.

Finally, when you are sure that all is correct, then clear your work area and arrange your tools so that they are comfortably to hand.

*Working Drawing, cutting grid – note the scale of four squares to one inch and see how there are five components in all.*

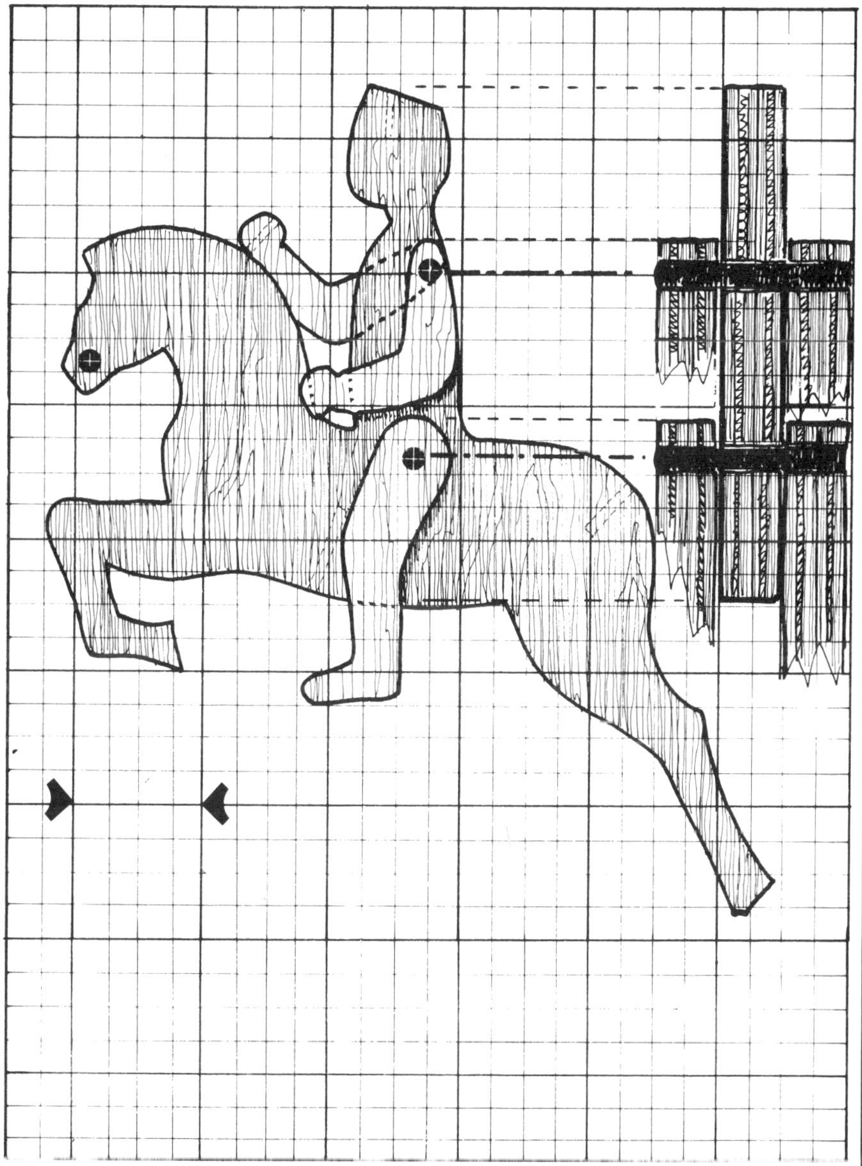

*Working Drawing, assembly grid —note the scale of four squares to one inch. See how the arms are dowel-fixed so that one is up and the other down.*

## CUTTING THE MULTIPLY

Once you have finalized the design, transferred it to the multiply, and marked out and clearly labelled all the various parts of the toy, then you are ready for the off. Set your wood up in the vice, or clamp it to the workbench, then using your chosen tool, be it a coping saw or whatever, carefully cut out the shapes. As you work, make sure that the cuts are at 90° to the surface of the ply, and aim for a sawn line that is crisp, smooth and clean edged.

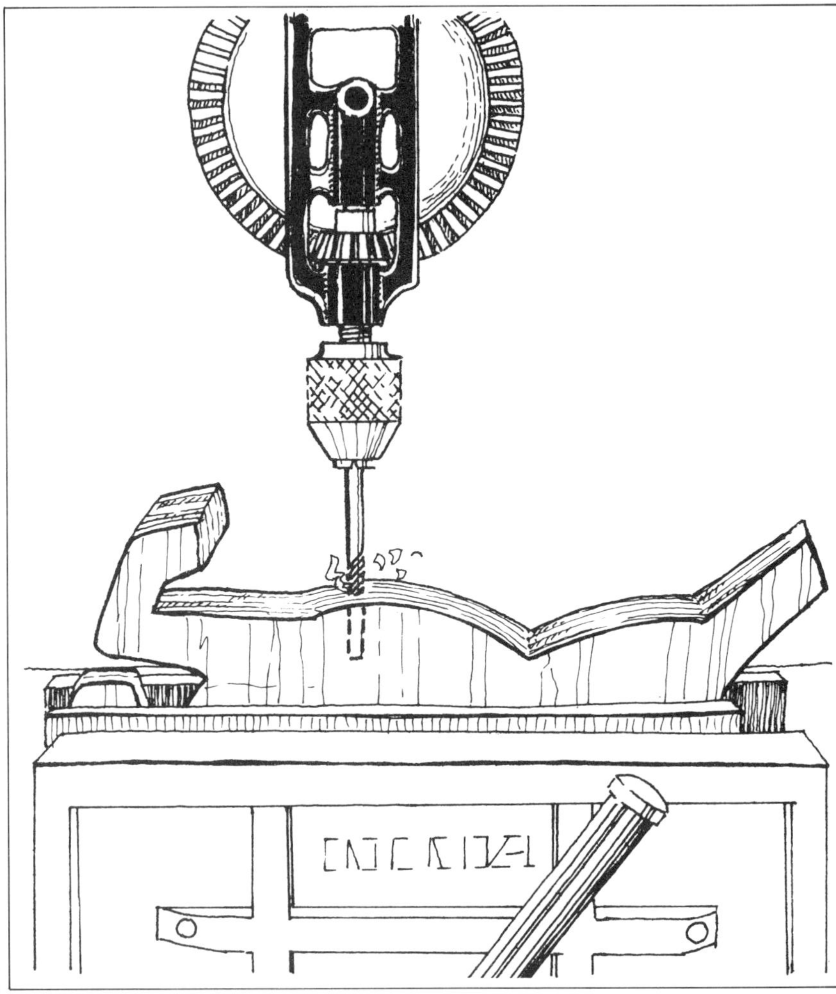

*Clamp the horse, belly up, in the vice, and drill the counterbalance wire hole —in this instance it is most important that the wire be at right angles to the cut edge of the wood, so make sure that the hole is well placed.*

We chose to work the wood with a small fine bladed coping saw, and must admit that many of our cuts are less than perfect. However this toy needs to look a little 'folksy' so a certain capriciousness of line and form is acceptable and even desirable.

## DRILLING THE PIVOT, WIRE AND TRIM HOLES

If you have a good look at the design layouts and detailed drawings, as illustrated, you will see that there are eleven holes in all: six pivotal, arm and leg swing holes that need to be worked with the ¼ inch drill bit and holes for the tail, reins, sabre, feather and counterbalance wire that can be worked with the ⅛ inch bit. When you drill these holes, use a wood waster or backing board so that you don't tear the wood, and try to keep the holes at 90° to the working face.

Finally, rub out and slightly countersink each of the holes with a scrap of sandpaper, and make sure that they are all free from burrs and rough edges.

## PREPARATION AND PAINTING

Take the graded sandpapers, and rub down all the components; that is to say, soften up all the cut angles and corners, and sand the cut edges until they are completely smooth to the touch. Note – if by chance, during the sawing or drilling, you damage the ply, fill the damaged area with high quality resin/hardener wood filler, then sand and make-good.

When you consider the various parts well rubbed down, give them several coats of white wood primer, rubbing down between coats, and then re-sand them to a fine finish.

Finally, when you reckon that all the parts are prepared, clear your work area, making sure that it's completely free from dust, then set out your paints, brushes, cleaners and cloths. Before you start painting, have a good long look at the inspirational drawings and any collected magazine clips, and have a few trial work-outs with scrap paper and felt tips. This done, mount the prepared ply shapes, as illustrated, or hang them on a wire grid, as shown in previous projects, then lay on a lump, run and blob free undercoat. When the undercoat is dry, give your chosen gloss enamel a last minute stir, then give all the toy parts a ground colour – say red for the Hussar's jacket, white for the horse, blue for the trousers and hat, and so on.

Finally, have a last look at your research and inspirational material, make sure the ground colour is dry, then pick out all the decorative, uniform and feature details with fine-line brush strokes. When you are painting, of course, the strokes need to be carefully considered, but try at the same time to keep them all bold, simple and direct, with plenty of sweeping curves and expressive thick and thin lines. Keep your wrists loose, only work with a fine-

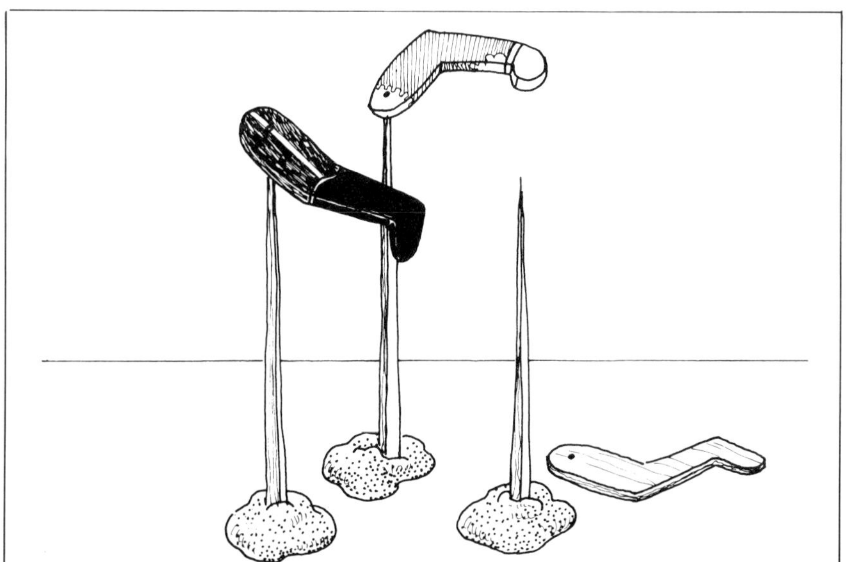

*When you come to painting, work out a system of holding or hanging the toy units while they are wet – we have used little splinters of wood and plasticine.*

pointed brush, and most important of all, avoid fussy, impossible to work detail.

## ASSEMBLY AND BRINGING TOGETHER

When all the toy parts have been painted, clear the worksurface, and be ready with the PVA glue. Now have yet another look at our working drawings, and see how the legs and arms of the Hussar are fixed to the hardwood rods, while the rods themselves are free to move within the pivotal holes.

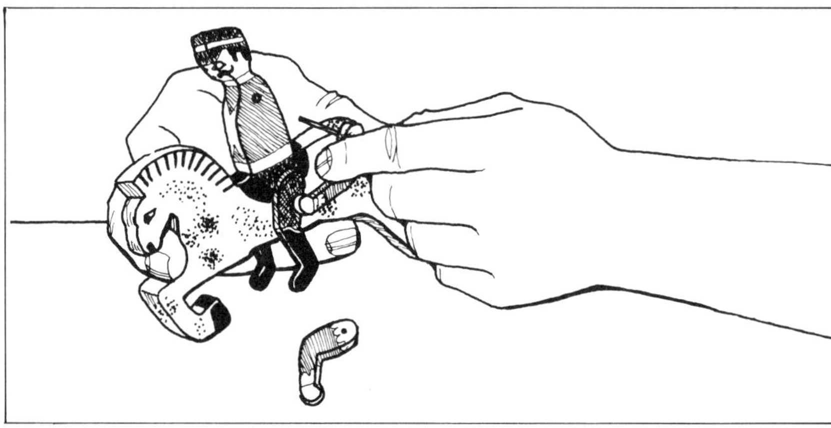

*When all the parts have been painted, position the limbs, slide home the dowels, and fix with small dabs of PVA glue.*

Clean out the rider/horse holes, then place, arrange and PVA glue the limbs, as illustrated. See how the Hussar's legs need to be fixed on the pivotal rod so that they are both at the same angle, and note how the arms are set one up and one down. Finally when the glue has set, make sure that the Hussar's arms and legs swing freely in their pivotal holes.

## THE COUNTERBALANCE WIRE BOB

If you look at our working drawings, you will see that we have used a shop-bought, lathe-made ball for the counterbalance; you might use a 'found' ball, a ball whittled from a scrap of hardwood, or even a flat ply shape; no matter, as long as the bob-weight counterbalances the horse. Take your length of coathanger wire, slide one end into the hole that you drilled in the horse's belly, and push the other end into the bob. This done, bend, curve, shape and shorten the wire, as you think fit, until the prancing horse maintains a nicely balanced stance. Note – our bob is about 2 inches in diameter, made of hardwood, and weighs a little under 1½ ounces.

It's a tricky business getting the counterbalance weight and wire just right, because after all they are both variables that are dictated by design choice and materials – if you run into problems, have a trial workout with scrap wire and plasticine. If you find, as we did, that the bob needs more weight, then maybe you could add lead shot, as illustrated. Finally, plug and make good any bob holes, and permanently fix the counterbalance wire with resin glue.

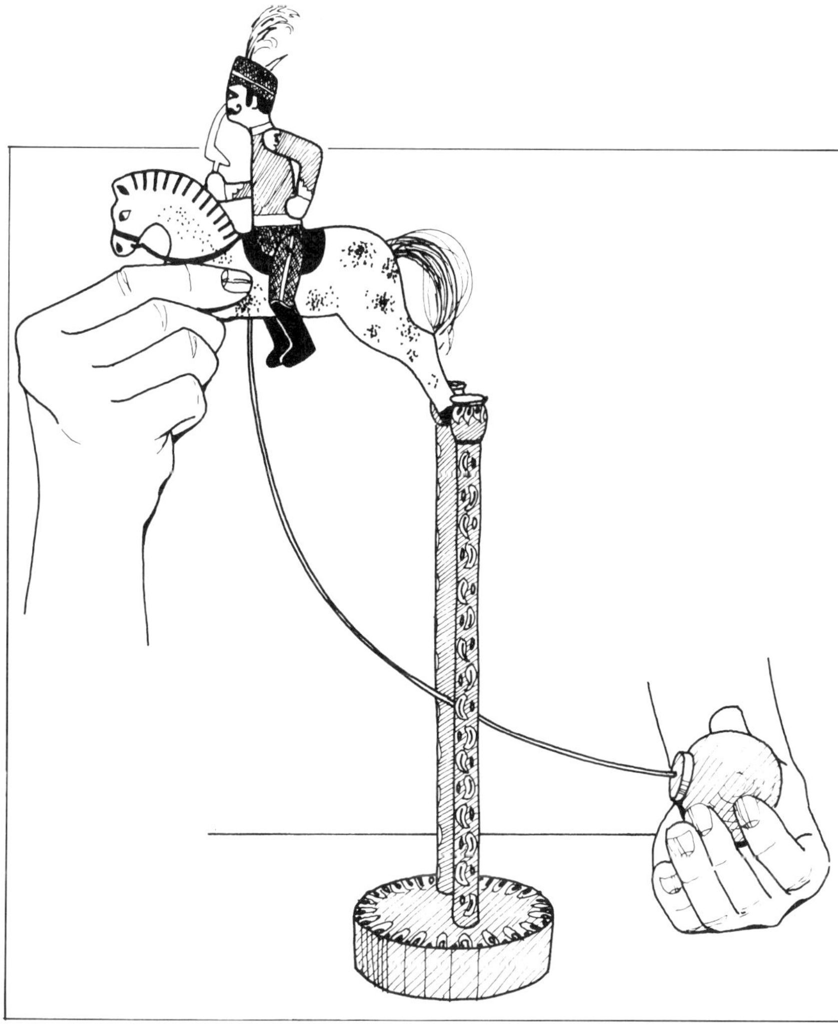

*The final wire and balance adjustment is a bit tricky; you might have to fiddle around for some time before you get it just right.*

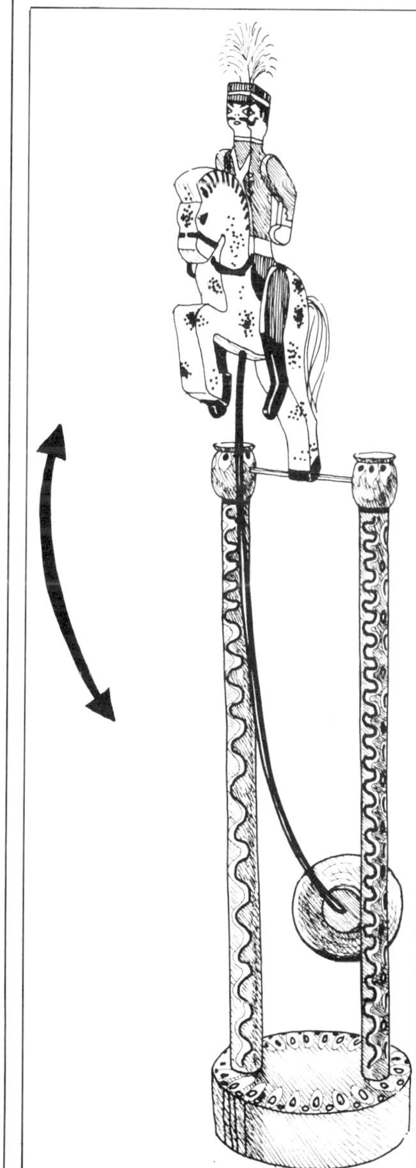

*In use, the counterbalance is carefully bent so that the Hussar is balanced – a little push and he will gently rock backwards and forwards.*

## THE STAND

Although this toy will balance very nicely on just about anything from a pin-head to the edge of say a shelf or table, it does without doubt look best arranged on a stand. We've seen stands that are turned, hand carved, whittled, wall-bracketed, square sectioned, made of metal, and so on. Our stand, as illustrated, is made up from two little turned posts and a 'found' disc of wood – the posts are about ½ inch thick, and the base to cross-wire height is about 12 inches.

## AFTERTHOUGHTS

Although our Hussar has a feather in his hat, and his horse is decorated with odds and ends of cord, brass and hardwood, there are of course a great many 'finish' possibilities; everything from highly ornate horse harness, to 'perfect in every detail' uniform insignia; we've even seen a horse and rider worked to perfect one twelfth scale.

This toy is worked in the flat – that is to say, the multiply has been left relatively sharp edged, but by building up the layers, and working with gouges and rasps, it is possible to work a toy that is rounded and sculptural.

Before you push the counterbalance wire into the horse's belly, tap it flat with a hammer, then it won't twist and upset the delicate counterbalance movement.

PROJECT EIGHT

# BUTTERFLY

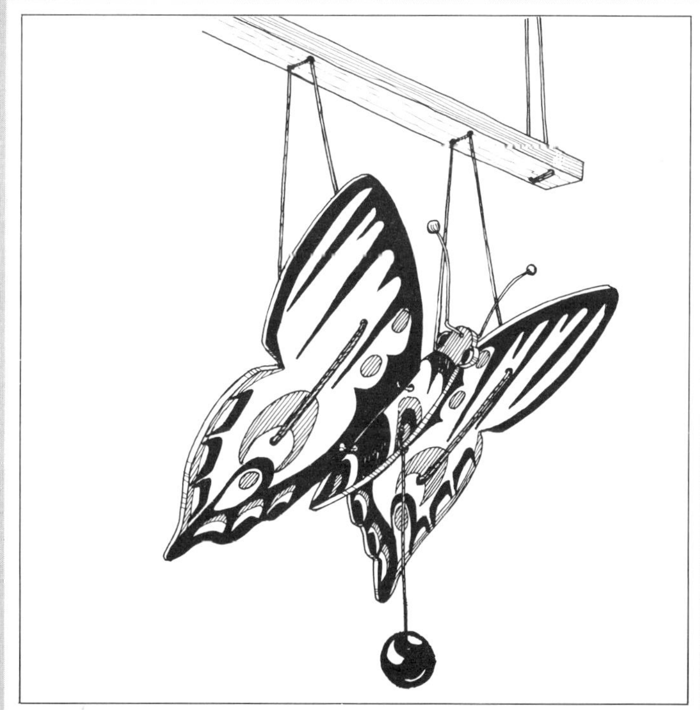

TOY TYPE · COUNTERBALANCE MOBILE

## THOUGHTS ON THE PROJECT

Is it a bird? Is it a plane? . . . No it's a simple-movement, counterbalance butterfly mobile. Now according to my prestigious encyclopedia come dictionary, . . . 'mobiles were invented in 1932 by the American artist sculptor Alexander Calder', . . . and it continues . . . 'a mobile is a sculpture suspended in mid air with delicately balanced parts that are set in motion by air currents'. All very helpful, . . . but as to being invented in the 1930's — surely not? We would say that the notion of decorative, wind-movement or

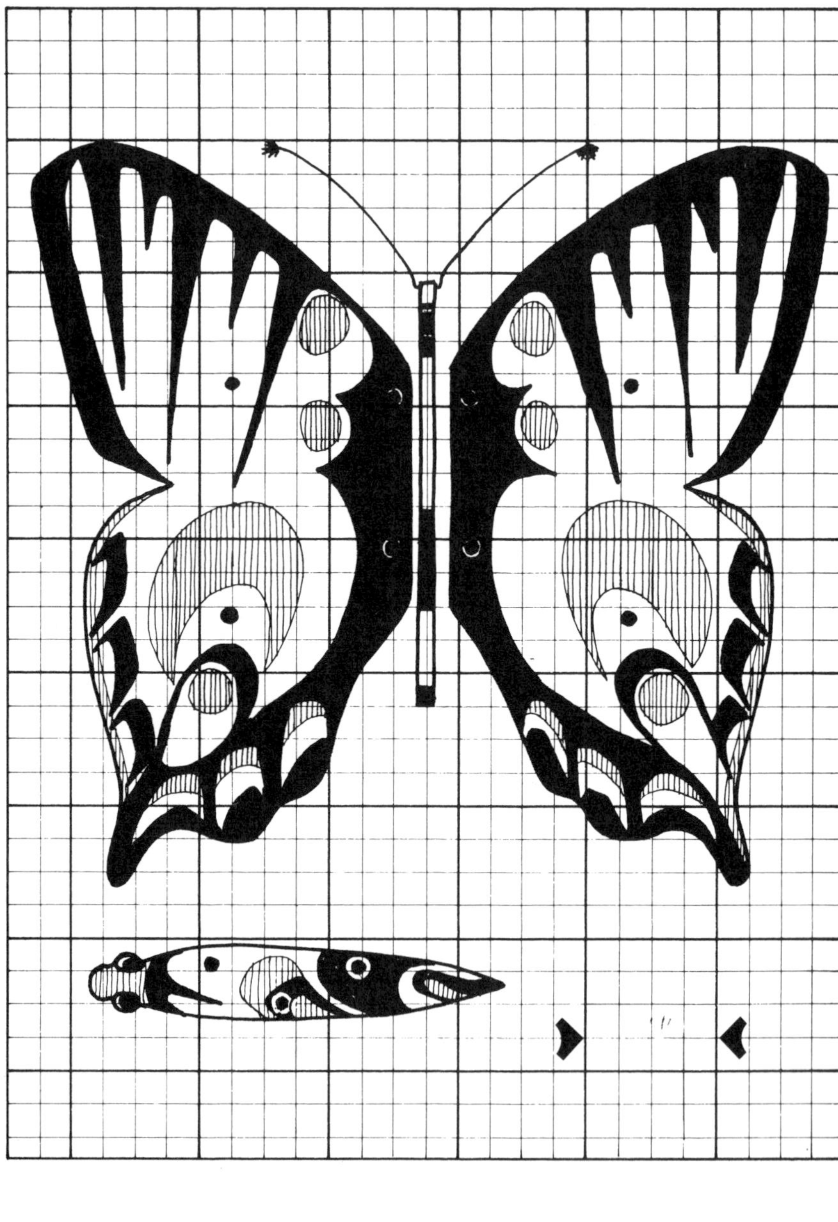

*Working Drawing, painting grid – note the scale of four squares to one inch. We have given the butterfly a stylized pattern, and also fitted a little spring-wire antenna.*

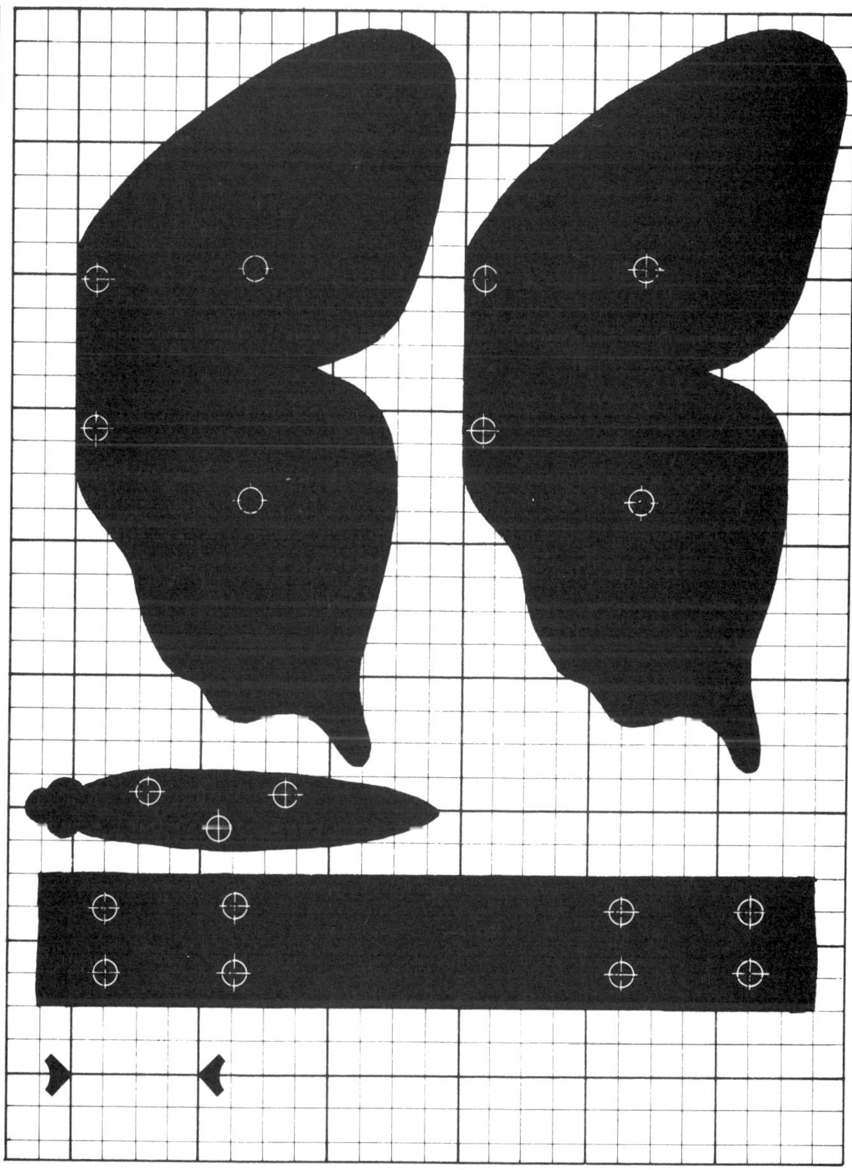

*Working Drawing, cutting grid – note the scale of four squares to one inch.*

air-current sculptures, toys and playthings goes way back. We've seen beautiful Polish, 'warm air' ceiling decorations made of straw, paper-cuts, dried peas, egg-shell and goose feathers. In Sweden, Switzerland and Denmark there is a tradition of making delicate hanging mobiles out of wood shavings and veneers; in Japan they make all manner of tissue and cane hangings; in China the folk artists make wood, glass and metal, wind operated, 'sound' decorations, and so we could go on ad infinitum.

We would say that mobile type toys are to be found where ever there is a craft tradition that involves wood, fine fabrics and delicate paper tissues.

Paper birds in Thailand, tissue butterflies in Indonesia, and so, no doubt, we could go on. However, all that apart, our interest in this toy was sparked off when we saw a brief reference to counterbalance mobiles in a couple of old American publications — a magazine and a pre-war book on wood carving. Of course, as is usually the way, the sketches were mere scribbles, and the counterbalance movement wasn't described.

Anyway, to get to the point, we were just beginning to work out a prototype, you know the sort of thing, acres of scrap card and miles of string and wire, when, would you believe, along comes a friend with a modern shop-bought, oriental, counterbalance bird toy. So there you have it — our butterfly must surely be a classic; its wings flutter in the lightest current of warm air, and its movement is totally realistic. Hang this toy in a child's playroom, or even in a sheltered garden, and it will give you, your family and friends hours of quiet pleasure.

## CONSIDERING THE PROJECT

When we first saw a brief reference to this butterfly counterbalance mobile in an old magazine, we must say it left us absolutely stone cold. How could such a delicate fragile creature as a butterfly find expression in a great clonking wooden toy? In fact we were so unimpressed that we decided to make our own working model, just to see if there was any substance in the claims that, . . . 'The movement of the butterfly is both wonderful and ingenious'. Well believe-you-me, this toy is a real beauty; don't take our word for it, much better to gather some scrap card and thread, and knock up your own prototype.

In the first instance, don't bother with carefully cut profiles and the like, just go for large broad shapes. Have a good look at the working drawings and details, and take special note of the position of the wing harness holes, the placing of the eight whiffletree or balance beam holes, and the precise arrangement of the harness cords. See also how the body of the butterfly counterbalances the wings, and how, in turn, the body is counterbalanced by its own carefully adjusted bob weight. You might say that this project hinges, both literally and metaphorically, on all the forms being precisely and nicely worked.

Finally, get to see pictures and magazine clips of large exotic moths and butterflies, and make design sketches of motifs, patterns and colours. Note — the scale of the working drawings is four grid squares to one inch.

## MATERIALS

For this project you need a piece of white faced, 1/8 inch thick multiply that measures about 7×9 inches, a large bead, or a collection of beads, or some such, for the counterbalance bob, two or three inches of springy hair-clip wire for the antennae, a couple of yards of nylon monofilament fishing line and finally you need a wood primer, an undercoat and a selection of brightly coloured model makers paints.

**Tools** As for tools, you need the use of a bench vice or clamp, a coping saw with some spare-blades, a hand drill with a 1/8 inch, or smaller, drill bit, a pack of graded sandpapers, a selection of shaped stick-tools to support the sandpaper, a pair of scissors, a fine-point, long haired paint brush, and, as with all the other projects, you need a whole heap of ordinary household tools like scrap paper, throw-away tubs, cloths and cleaners.

## SETTING OUT THE DESIGN AND CUTTING THE PLY

Run your eye over our scale drawings and note the measurements — 6¼ inches from wing-tip to wing-tip, about 3 inches from nose to tail, a fore-to-aft wing length of about 5–6 inches and a balance beam that measures 6×1

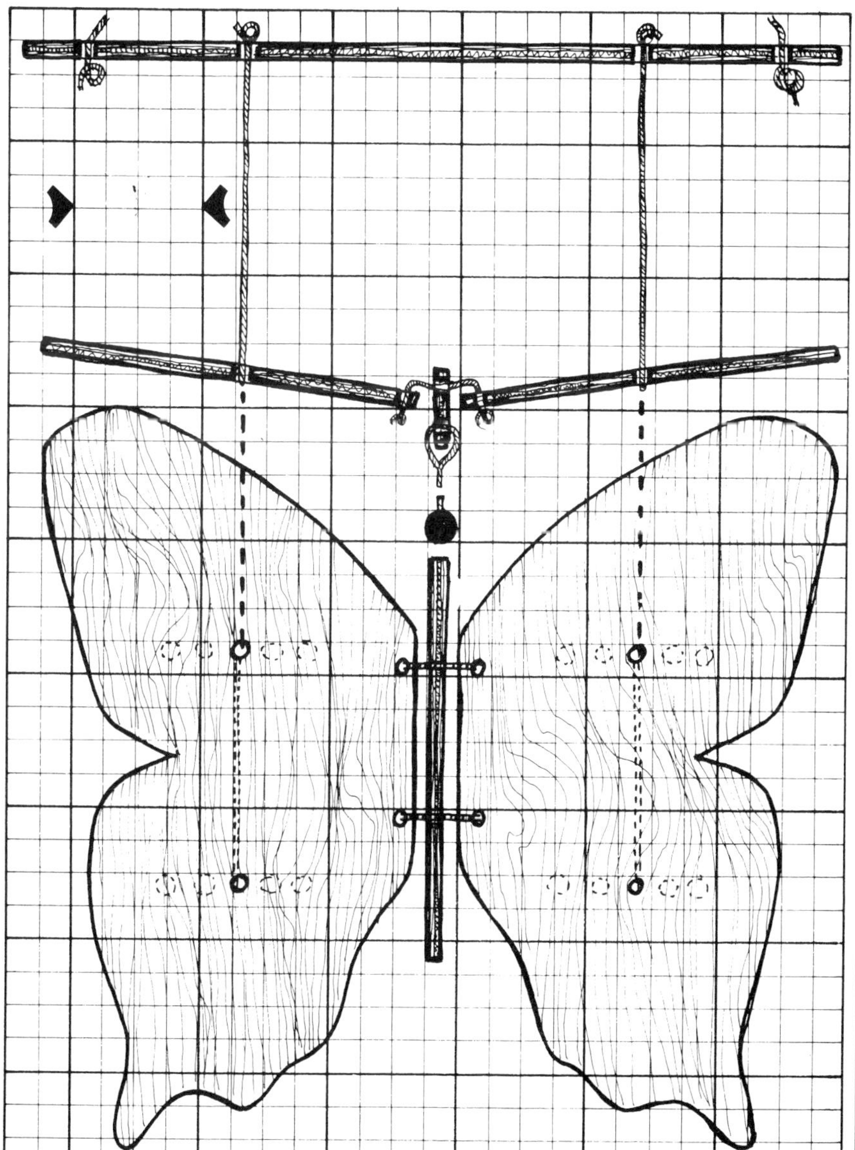

*Working Drawing, assembly grid – note the scale of four squares to one inch. See how the wings are fixed to the body, and how 'at rest' the harness strings are parallel to each other – note also the wing dihedral angle, and the wing-tip distance of about ¼–½ inch from level.*

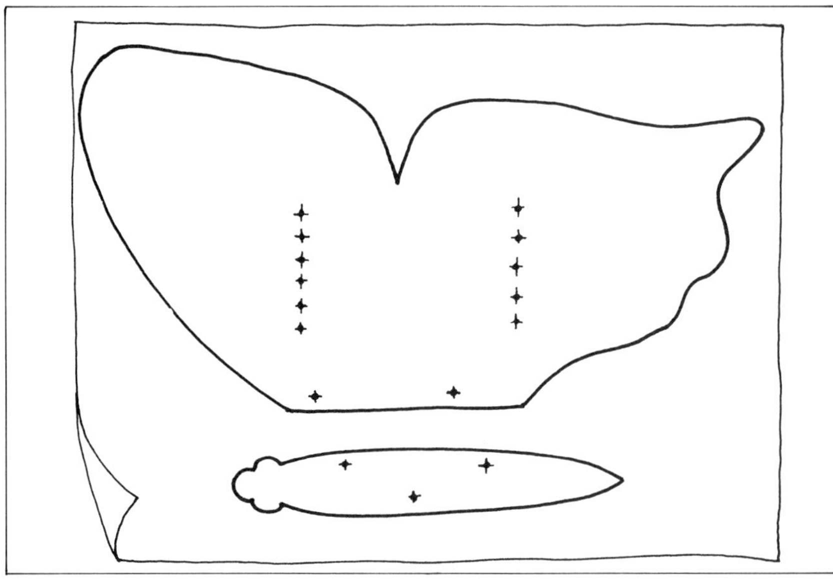

*Trace the lines of the design, and then pencil press transfer the lines through to the working face of the wood.*

inch. Now take some scrap paper and work out what you consider to be an exciting stylized butterfly motif/profile.

When you have achieved a good workable design, take a tracing, and then pencil press transfer the lines of the design through to the working face of the wood. This done, take a 2B pencil and carefully establish the transferred lines. Now set the wood in the vice, take a coping saw, and fret out the four drawn shapes: the two wings, the body and the whiffletree.

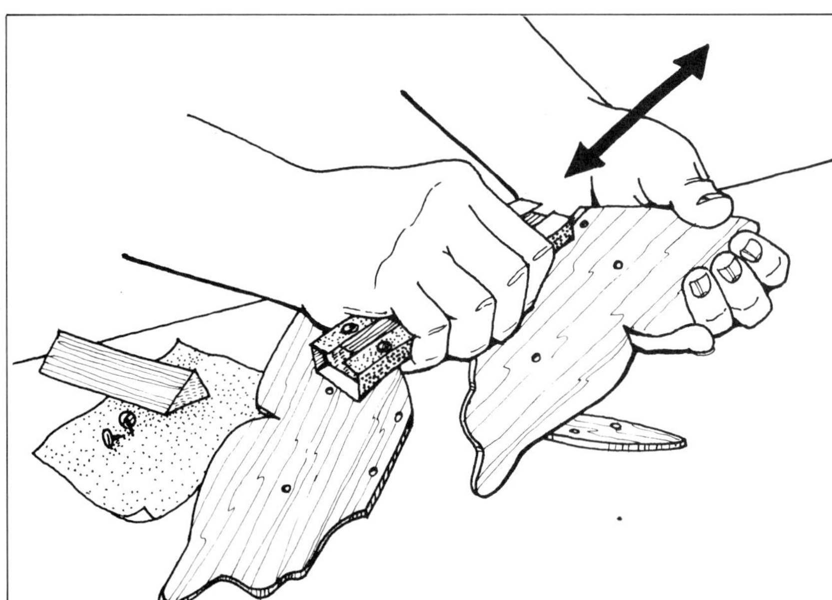

*Support the sandpaper with shaped stick-tools, then rub down cut edges of the wood until they are smooth.*

## DRILLING AND RUBBING DOWN

When you have fretted the wood, cleared the work surface of all the scrap, and arranged all your tools so that they are to hand, then have a look at our working drawings, and note the position of the various drilled holes. The body-to-wing holes are no problem; they are about 1 inch apart and about 1/8 inch in from the edge of the ply; the wing harness holes on the other hand are a bit tricky and need thinking about. If you look at our 'section' working drawings you will see that although in each wing there are only two drilled holes, we have also indicated, with dotted circles, other possible hole positions. The thinking behind this is the fact that the precise placing of the holes depends on several variables, the weight of your wood, the air resistance, the wing area and so on. So with this in mind, you can either drill five holes at each harness point, then use one, and fill the rest, or you can make the drilled holes all part and parcel of the overall design.

However, when you have established the position of the holes, take your drill, support the wood with a backing waster board, and then work the holes. This done, take your shaped stick-tools and sandpaper, and work the wood to a nice smooth round-edged finish.

Now at this stage, it might be as well to have a trial 'stringing', just to see if the various harness and link holes are in the correct position. And so you hang the balance beam from the ceiling, knot-on the body and wings, and then hang the butterfly from the beam, all as illustrated.

This done, knock-up a temporary bob weight counterbalance out of plasticine and string, and adjust the bob until the dihedral angle between the body and wing raises the wing tips up 3/8 inch from the horizontal (see working drawings). Finally, when you reckon that all is correct, take notes and sketches, then dismantle the butterfly and weigh the counterbalance bob.

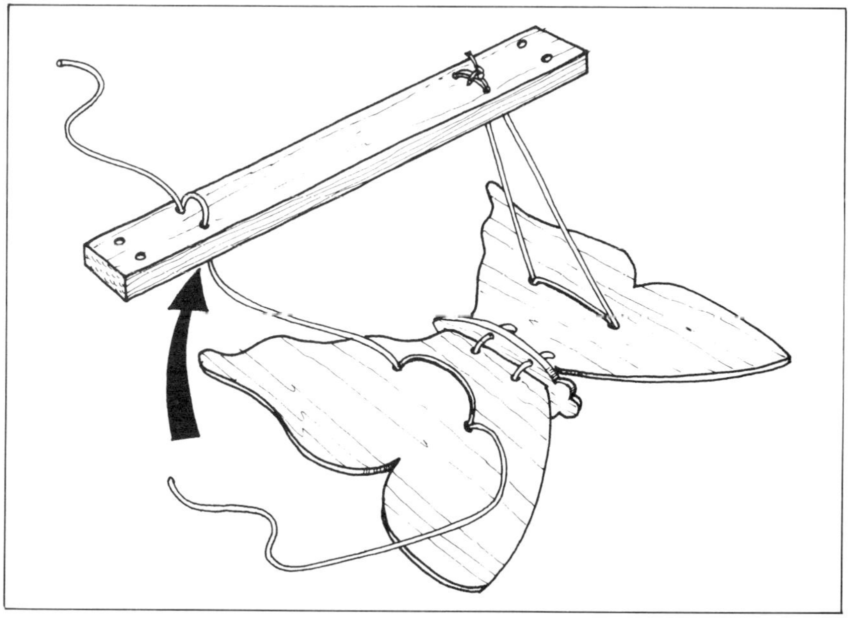

*When the butterfly has been cut out, have a trial stringing-up just to make sure that all is correct. You might need to re-position the wing holes.*

*When the components have been gloss painted, and the paint is dry, trace and transfer the lines of the wing patterns to the painted wood.*

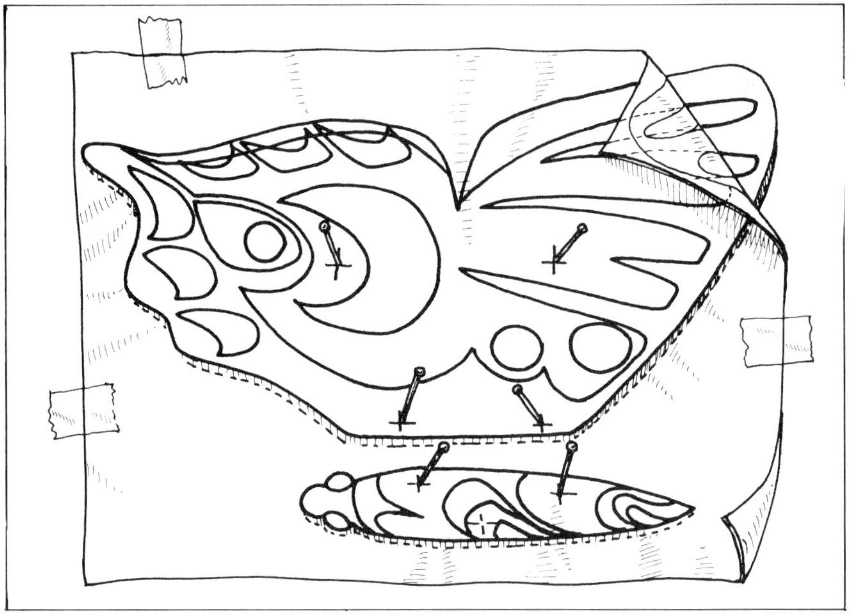

## PAINTING AND STRINGING UP

Clear away all the bench clutter and wood dust, or better still work in a special painting area, then set out the butterfly and all your painting materials. Note — of all the toys in this book, we would say that the butterfly has the most decorative potential, so take time researching the patterns and motifs. Work out a good vigorous bold design, then make full size colour and reference drawings.

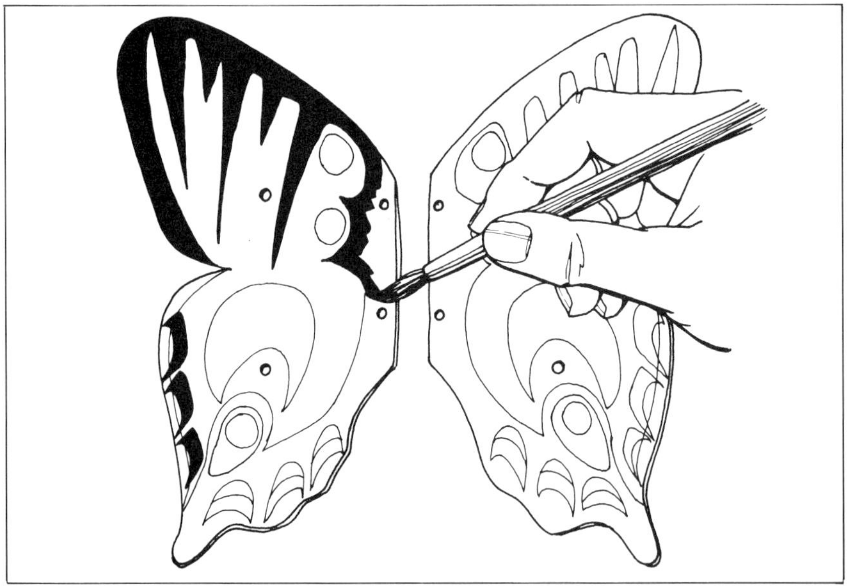

*Painting a delicate and complex design of this character can be tricky, so work at it slowly, use a fine brush, and edge in the motifs.*

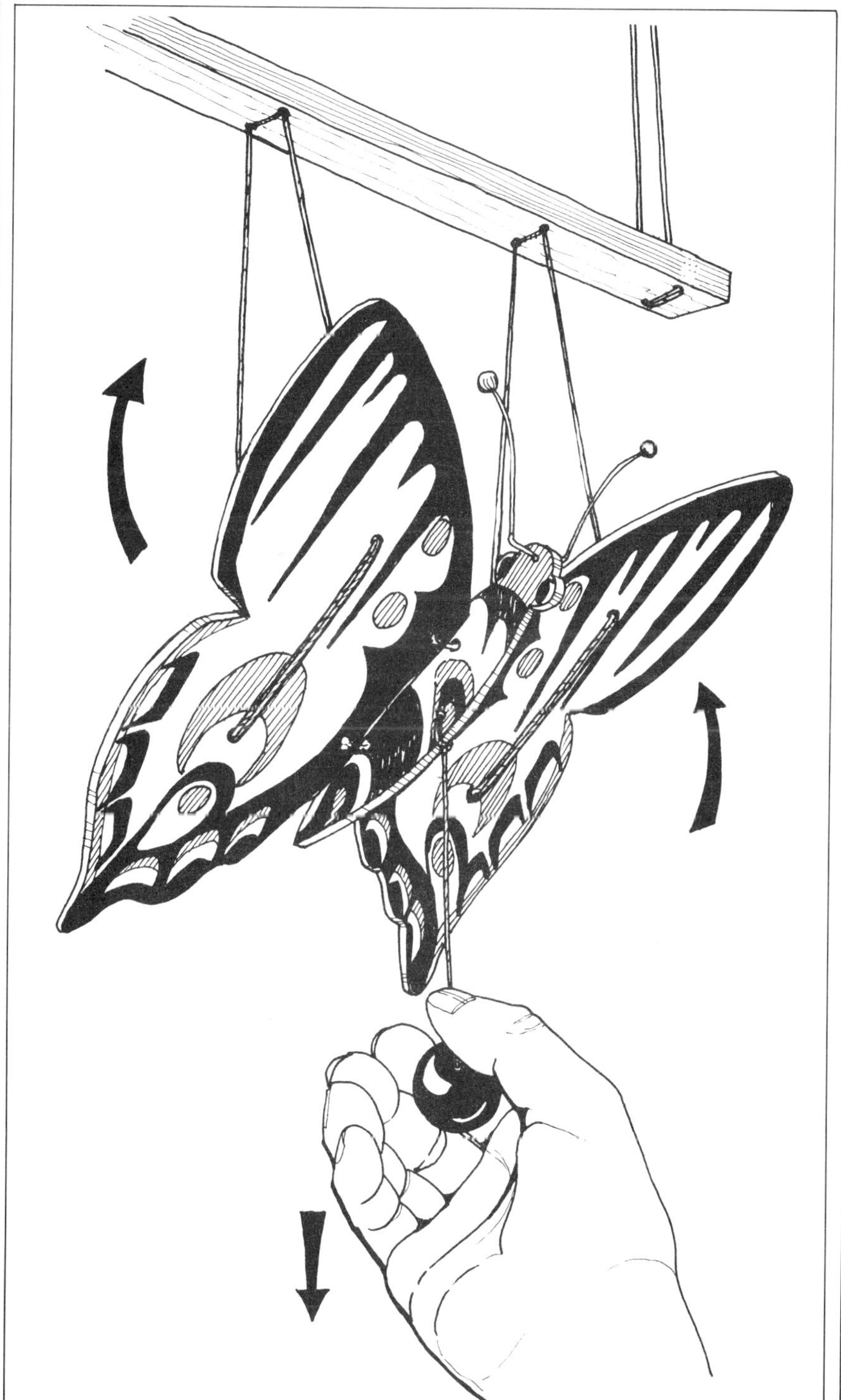

*In use the butterfly is hung from the ceiling so that it catches wafts of warm air. With a little encouragement the wings of the butterfly will gently flap up and down with a most realistic movement.*

Now lay on a primer and an undercoat, then, when the undercoat has been dried and rubbed down, lay on the main gloss coat. When this ground coat has dried, transfer the lines of the butterfly patterns to the painted wood, then take the fine-point brush and pick out all the multicoloured details. Now wait a while for the paint to dry, refer back to your stringing-up notes, then take the nylon line and rig up the butterfly harness, as already described and shown. Finally knot-on a suitably weight-adjusted bob, make good any scratches and the job is done.

## AFTERTHOUGHTS

If you decide to scale up the butterfly, then all well and good; you still use 1/8 inch ply, but if you want to scale down, and make a butterfly that is say only an inch or two across, then use a delicate wood veneer.

When you are putting the butterfly together, work it so that there is about an 1/8 inch gap between the body and the wings, then you won't have any problems with wood-to-wood friction.

When you are rigging the butterfly, make sure that you run the nylon line twice through all holes, and double knot and heat seal all line ends. Note that we refer to the balance beam as a 'whiffletree', meaning a crossbar to which lines are attached as with a horse harness.

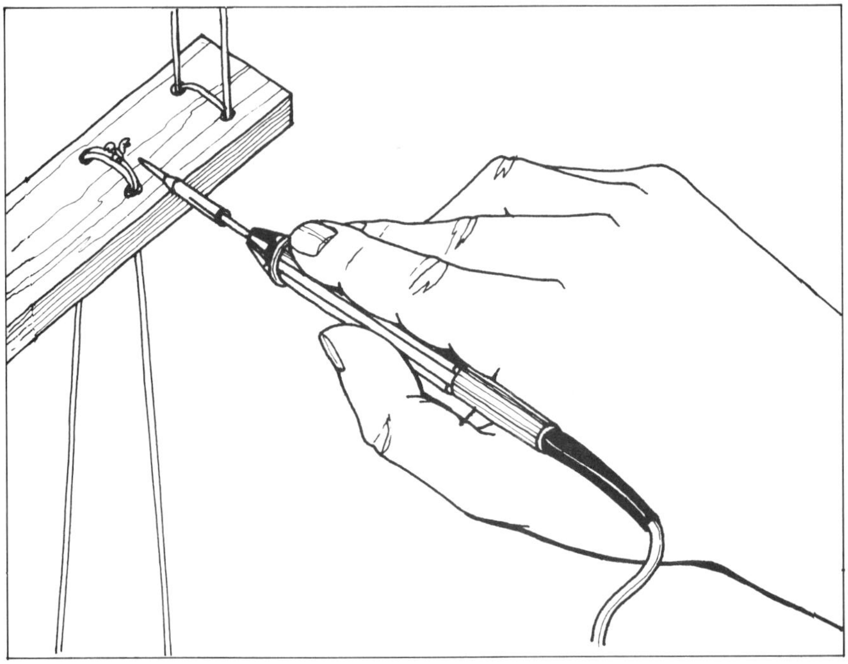

*Make sure all the harness knots are well placed and secure, then blob-fix them with a hot soldering iron.*

PROJECT NINE

# PETER THE POUNCING CAT

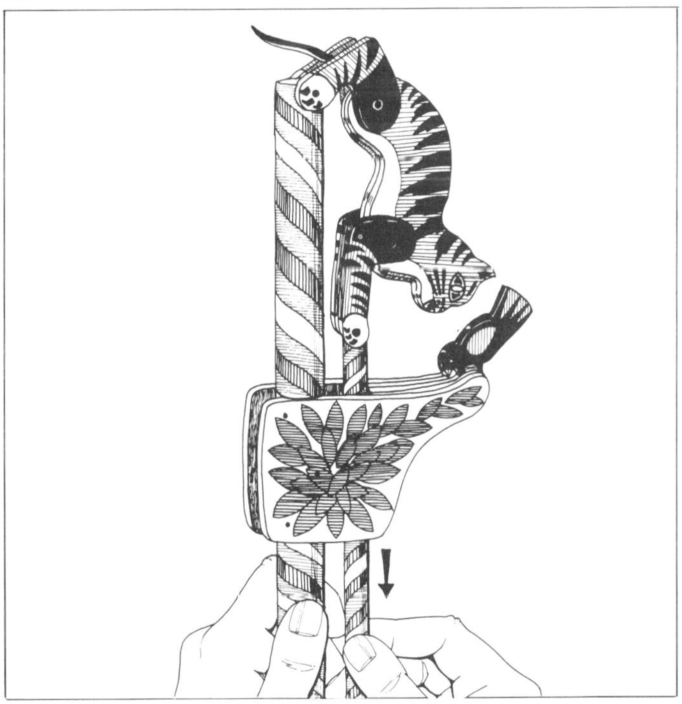

TOY TYPE · PIVOTAL LIMBS AND STICKS

## THOUGHTS ON THE PROJECT

Cat-up-a-stick, Monkey-up-a-tree and Admiral-up-mast; all belong to the same toymaking tradition in that they were 'country', 'peasant' or 'folk' made, and worked from whittled, carved and painted wood. Toys of this type are all of a kind; that is to say, they were made to be sold at the great fairs, they were sold for as little as a penny and they were designed so that they had ingenious moving parts. Described variously as, 'Penny Fairings', 'Black Forest Mechanical', or even just 'simple-movement', toys of this character were made all over Europe.

If you could go back in time and space to the pre-industrial period, when it was a big adventure to travel the ten or so miles to the next village or small town, and you could search out a handful of typical English, German, Russian or Polish rural communities, you would find, as likely as not, that they all had long established traditions of making wooden toys. Of course there's no great mystery as to 'why?' or 'how?', the answer is simple enough – these poor peasant, 'close to the earth' communities needed to supplement their economy – what better way of putting time and talent to good use, than making small craft items out of locally found materials? And so it was that many pre-twentieth century cottagers, be they English, Russian, Austrian or whatever, spent the long winter evenings carving and whittling the local wood and making all manner of simple movement toys.

To really apppreciate just how clever some of these toys are, you need to see them in action. With this particular on-a-stick toy, the two sticks are held, one in each hand, and then the jointed animal is operated by sliding the sticks up and down. Now the amazing thing is, when the jointed form, be it a monkey, cat or man, slides over the end of the moving sticks, he appears to be performing the most beautiful sinuous acrobatics.

If you look at our toy, as illustrated, you will see that although we have stayed with the traditional two-stick-and-figure form, we have taken the design a little further and modified the stick-band so that the cat looks to be stalking, or about to pounce on, a bird. See also how the stick-band is fixed to the larger of the two sticks, and how the slender stick is free to move up and down within the confines of the band.

## CONSIDERING THE DESIGN

It might be as well with this project, especially if you haven't seen the toy in action, to gather a few scraps of card, wood and string, and see if you can put together a working model or prototype. In the first instance stay with our design and general dimensions, get the toy working, and discover just how it is operated. See how one stick can be held still while the other is moved, or how both sticks can be joggled simultaneously.

Now look at the working drawings and cutting grid, and note how this project uses the $^{3}/_{16}$ inch multiply – that is laminating two layers for the cat's body, and five layers for the bird and stick-band. When we were working on the prototype we considered using all sorts of materials, wire for the smaller of the two sticks, metal twist-screw eyelets, and so on. However after a deal of thought, and bearing in mind child safety factors, we decided to go for a sound, uncomplicated all-wood toy.

*In use, the two sticks are held, one in each hand, then they are joggled up and down so that the cat appears to slide over the top of the fat stick.*

Finally, before you start work, collect inspirational pictures and magazine clips, and maybe also visit a toy museum. Note — after seeing traditional, 'up-a-stick' toys, you may feel that you can improve upon our design.

## MATERIALS

For this project you need a piece of white faced $^3/_{16}$ inch multiply that measures about 9 × 9 inches, two 12 inch long dowels, one at $^3/_8$ inch and the other at $^3/_4$ inch, six brass panel pins or small screws, white PVA wood glue, about 8 inches of $^1/_4$ inch hardwood dowel, a selection of model makers enamel paints, colours to suit, a few scraps of dress-leather for the tail, a white wood primer, an undercoat, and of course you also need such general items as sandpaper, workout paper and tracing paper.

*Working Drawing, painting grid – note the scale of four squares to one inch – all to be painted in brilliant primary colours.*

*Working Drawing, cutting grid – note the scale of four squares to one inch —there are thirteen units in all.*

**Tools** You need the use of a bench or table clamp, a coping, jig, fret or band saw, a hand drill with a ¼ inch drill bit, a selection of shaped stick tools to use with the sandpaper, a small knife, a metal straight edge, fine and large soft haired brushes, and a pack of felt tip pens.

## SETTING OUT THE DESIGN AND CUTTING THE MULTIPLY

Referring to our drawing grids, and using workout and tracing paper, pencils and felt tips, design and set-out the various elements of the toy. See how our toy has thirteen cut-ply parts in all: two cat bodies, four legs, two hind-leg washers, two stick-band side plates, two stick-band distance pieces and a single bird piece. Note the scale of our working drawings is four grid squares to one inch.

Once you reckon that you have a good working design, be it ours or a modification of your own, take a tracing, and then pencil press transfer the lines of the design through to the working face of your $^{3}/_{16}$ inch multiply. This done, set your wood up in the vice, or clamp it to the workbench, take your chosen saw and carefully fret out the various shapes.

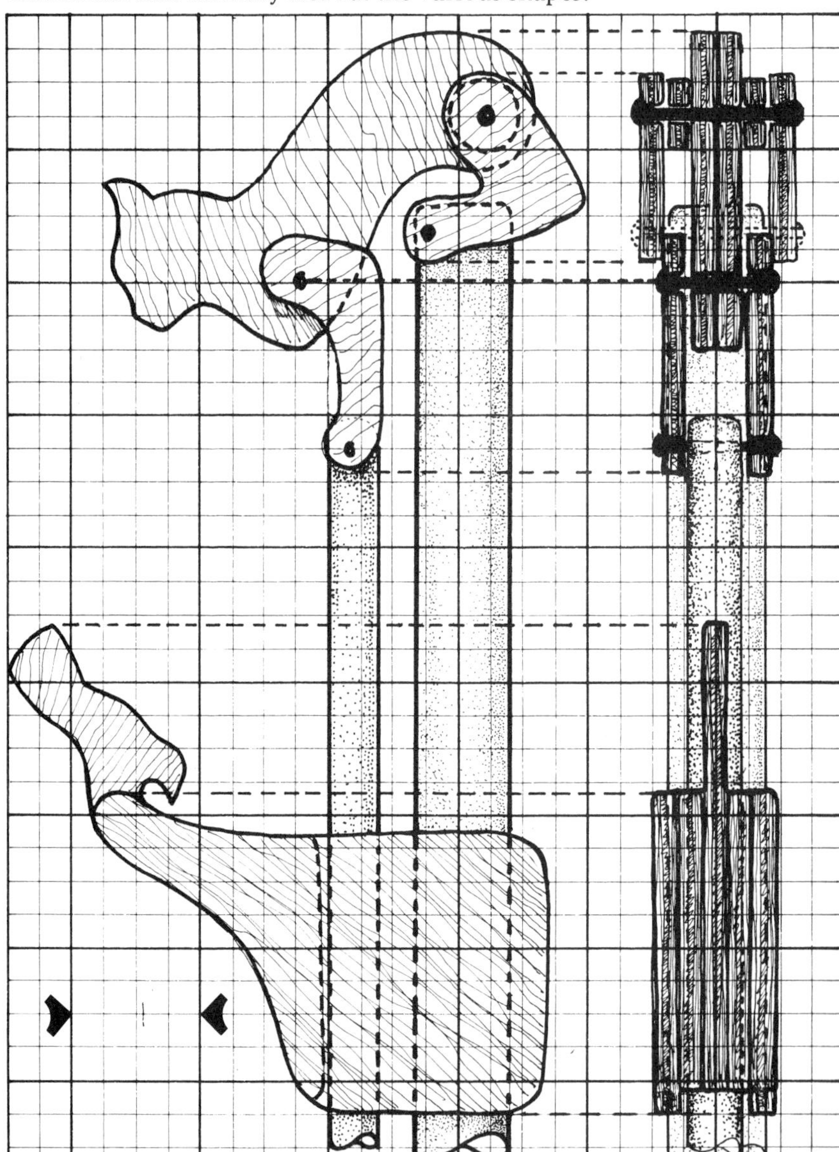

*Working Drawing, assembly grid – note the scale of four squares to one inch. See how the cat's back legs are spaced out, or packed out with washers so that they fit each side of the fatter of the two dowel-sticks.*

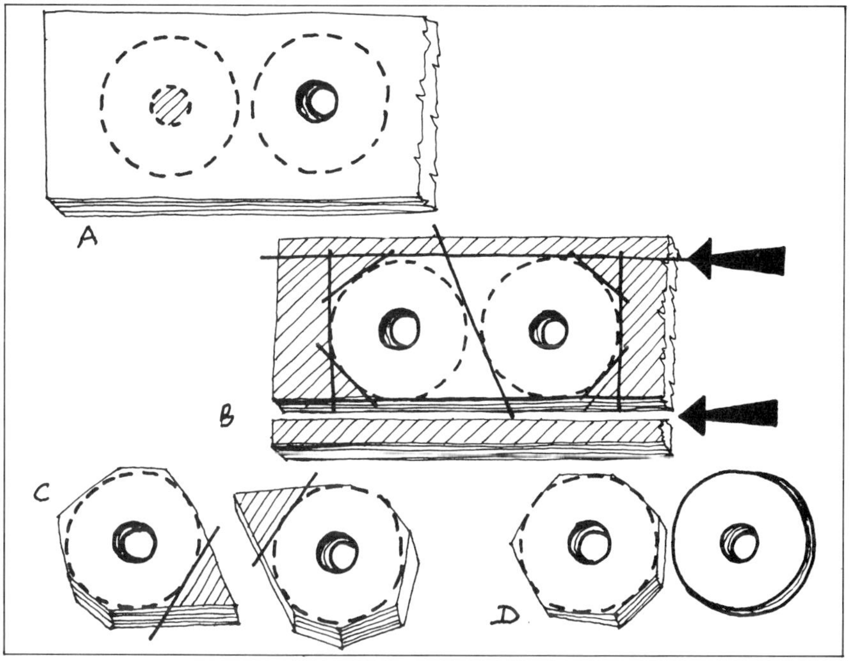


*Making wooden washers, (a) mark out the discs and drill central pivot holes. (b) cut away unwanted lumps of wood. (c) cut close to the required circle outline. (d) finally sand and rub down to a smooth roundness.*

When you are cutting the ply, try to keep the saw blade straight to the working face of the wood, and watch out that you don't tear the delicate layers of face wood. If you look at our drawings, layouts and details, you will see that in some instances we have grouped ply shapes so that they more or less share the same cutting line — we've done this for reasons of economy.

## CUTTING AND WORKING THE STICKS

Cut yourself two 12 inch long sticks or dowels, one at 3/8 inch diameter and the other at 3/4 inch, then take a knife and sandpaper and work them until they are smooth and round ended. Note — if you want to cut costs, you could make the two sticks from cheaper square sectioned wood.

## PLACING, GLUING AND LAMINATING

Take all the cut pieces of wood and set them out on the worksurface so that you have three groups — that is to say, two sticks, the pieces that make up the cat, and the pieces that go to make up the bird and stick-band. Now have a trial placing, and check all the pieces and parts for general size and fit. Getting the cat together is simple enough; the front legs sit each side of the cat's body, and the cats hind legs are distanced by the two washers. The stick-band isn't so straightforward, so have a long look at the working drawings and sections, and see how the side plates are pinned and glued to the 3/4 inch stick, and how the bird, distance pieces and side plates, go to make a stick channel and a total five-ply lamination thickness of about 1 inch.

When you are satisfied that all the elements are of a good size and fit, clear

*Take all the bits of ply that make up the stick-band, smear them with PVA glue, place them in the correct order, then put them in a clamp.*

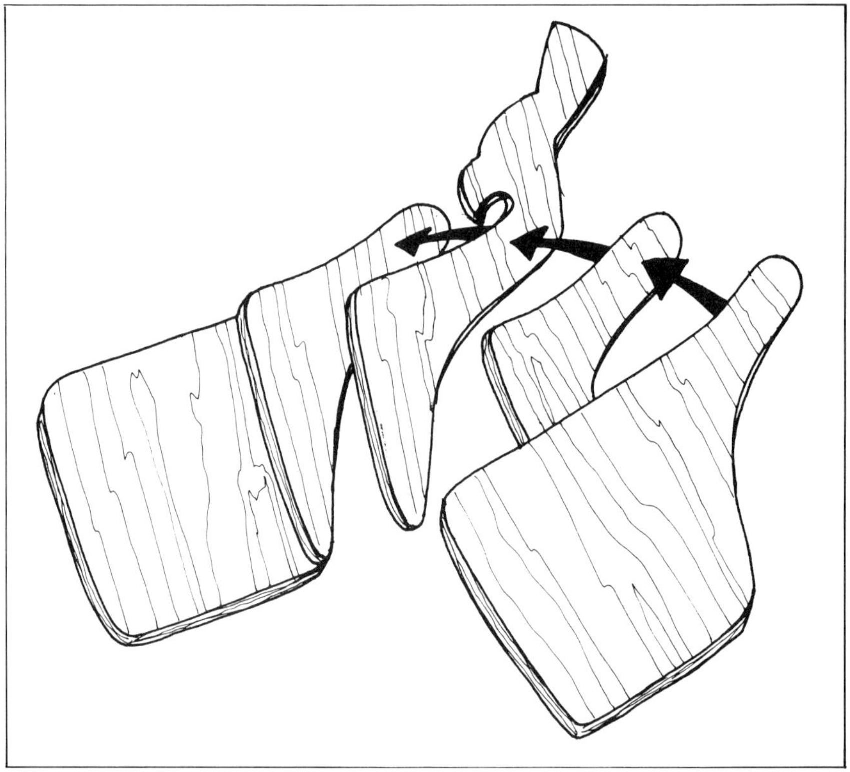

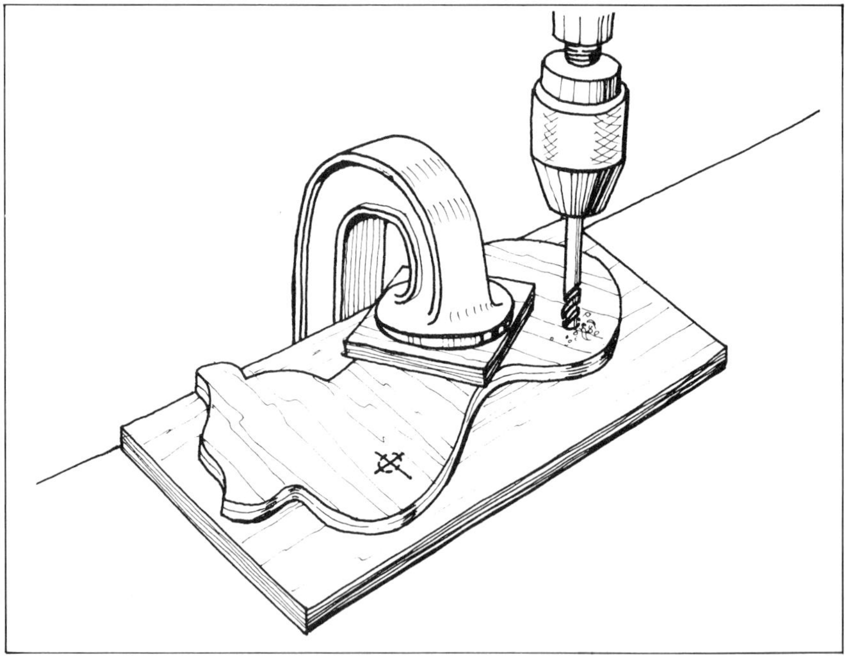

*When you have established just where all the holes ought to be, place the wood in a clamp, and then set-to with the drill.*

the worksurface and be ready with the PVA glue and clamps. Glue and clamp the two cat bodies together so that you have a single wood thickness of $^3/_8$ inch, then glue and clamp, as illustrated, the five elements that go to make up the stick-band.

## DRILLING, RUBBING DOWN AND PAINTING

When the glue is dry, say after twenty-four hours or so, take the hand drill and the ¼ inch drill bit, and work the pivotal holes in the cat, two in each of the four legs, in the washers, and at the end of the sticks; there should be fourteen holes in all. This done, take the graded sandpapers and work all the wood until it is completely round cornered, smooth edged, crisp and free from burrs. When you come to sanding the holes, make sure that those in the legs stay at ¼ inch, but work all the others so that they are a loose fit over the ¼ inch hardwood dowel. Now have another dry fitting together of all the parts, and see how the toy moves and works. When you are sure that all is correct, dust off your wood, and take a damp cloth and make sure that all your worksurfaces are clean.

Before you start painting, decide how you are going to support the bits of toy when they have been painted. That is to say, are you going to hang them on a wire grid with string ties? are you going to use a line, pins and cottons? Get your work area well set up and organized, and make sure that all your paints, brushes, cloths and cleaners are all to hand. Give the wood a generous priming, and one or two undercoats, depending on the quality of finish that you need, then lay on a thin topcoat.

Finally, when the enamel ground colours are dry, take a fine point brush

*First paint and decorate all the components and let the paint dry, then take the back and front legs and place them at the top of the sticks.*

and pick out the motif details: the eyes, the whiskers, the patterns on the cat, the maypole stripes round the two sticks, the bird and leaves, and so on.

## BRINGING TOGETHER AND WORKING AND GLUING THE PIVOT RODS

Cut the 1/4 inch hardwood dowel into four 2 inch lengths, and then be ready with the knife, the brass pins and a small tack hammer. Put the toy together, as illustrated; that is with two rods linking the cat's paws to the top of the sticks, rods linking the limbs and washers to the cat's body, and the bird/stick-band being held in place with glue and pins, on the 3/4 inch stick

*When the legs/paws are in position, place the body and back-leg washers.*

Now the next stage is tricky, so go easy and take it a step at a time. Cut the dowel lengths closer to size, cut and split the dowel ends, then very carefully take eight little slices of hardwood, and glue and wedge the dowel ends so that they are a tight fit within the limb holes. This done, slide the bird-band over the two sticks, and fix it, as shown, with glue and pins.

Finally, carefully knife-trim the dowel ends and the toy is finished. Now for the big moment — take the two sticks, one in each hand, and jiggle them up and down; if the cat slides over the top of the slender stick, and comes to halt about 1/4 inch or so from the bird, then the toy is a success.

## AFTERTHOUGHTS

If you have doubts about the split and wedge-end dowel rods, and think that they might be a bit of a problem, you could use brass nuts and bolts, metal or

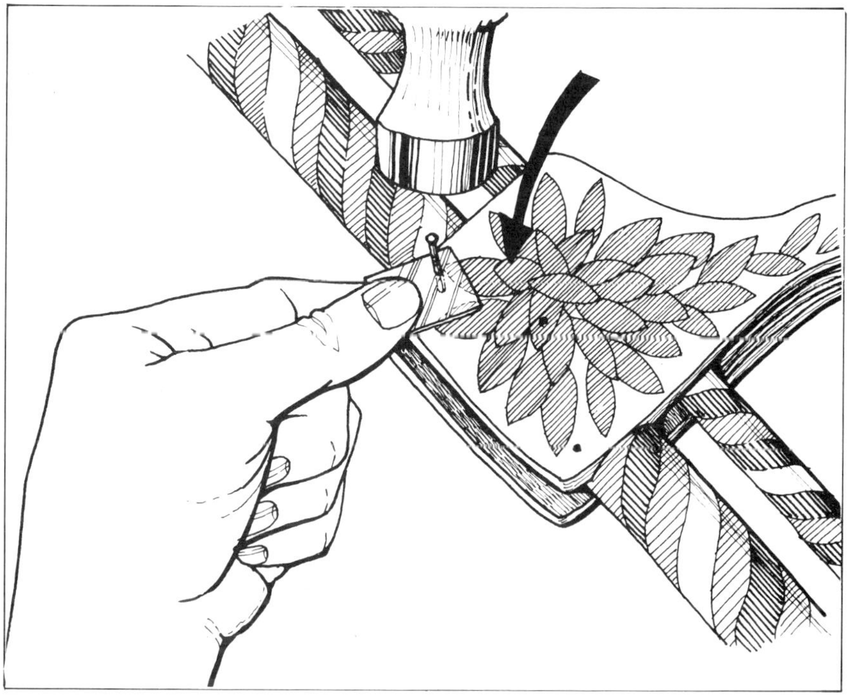

*Now place the stick-band in position, then using a little scrap of clear plastic to help you hold the pins, nail-fix it to the fatter of the two dowels.*

wood dowels with split pins, or even washers and crushed-end soft metal pins — see the section at the beginning of the book.

When you are working the initial design, bear in mind that it is possible to

*Finally, when the cat has been well placed, cut the dowels to size, slit the dowel ends, glue the slits and tap home the wedges.*

use a variety of materials, say ½ inch ply for the cat's body, sticks made out of square section wood, etc. However, if you do want to adjust our designs, then it's all the more important that you make a prototype, just to make sure your modifications work.

The cat body and stick-top holes do need to be a loose fit on the ¼ inch hardwood dowel, so after the painting stage, have another test fitting.

When we were at the design stage, we thought about working the project so that as the cat came over the top of the stick, the bird moved backwards — maybe you could use strings, a cam, or a flick-and-release catch, and work this feature into your design — it's a thought!

When you are painting, always stir, mix and use the paints as described by the manufacturer. Let the paint dry between coats, rub down the wood between coats, and never use a paint unless you are completely sure that it is non-toxic.

PROJECT TEN

# THE CRUNCHY CROC

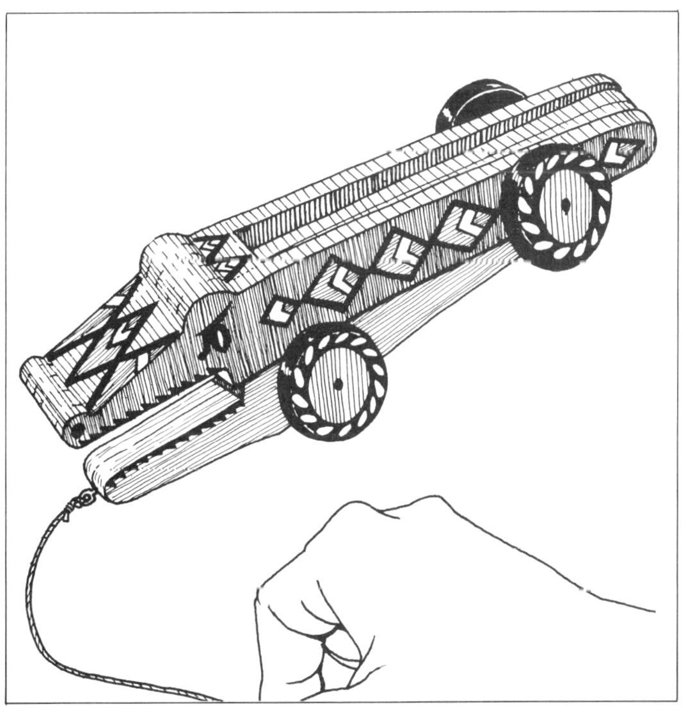

TOY TYPE · A PULL-ALONG CROCODILE WITH CAM OPERATED JAWS

## THOUGHTS ON THE PROJECT

When I was a little nipper, I suppose about five or six years old, my favourite toy was a wooden, pull-along dog. As I remember, he was called 'Dimby' or 'Dobby' – he looked a bit like a terrier; he had four stiff legs, two of which were broken and his face was a mess – he was altogether beautiful! But the thing that I liked best about this poor beaten and splintered beast was the fact that as I dragged him around the house, his hinged lower jaw opened and closed with much clonking and clunking; or, as I imagined at the time, with a

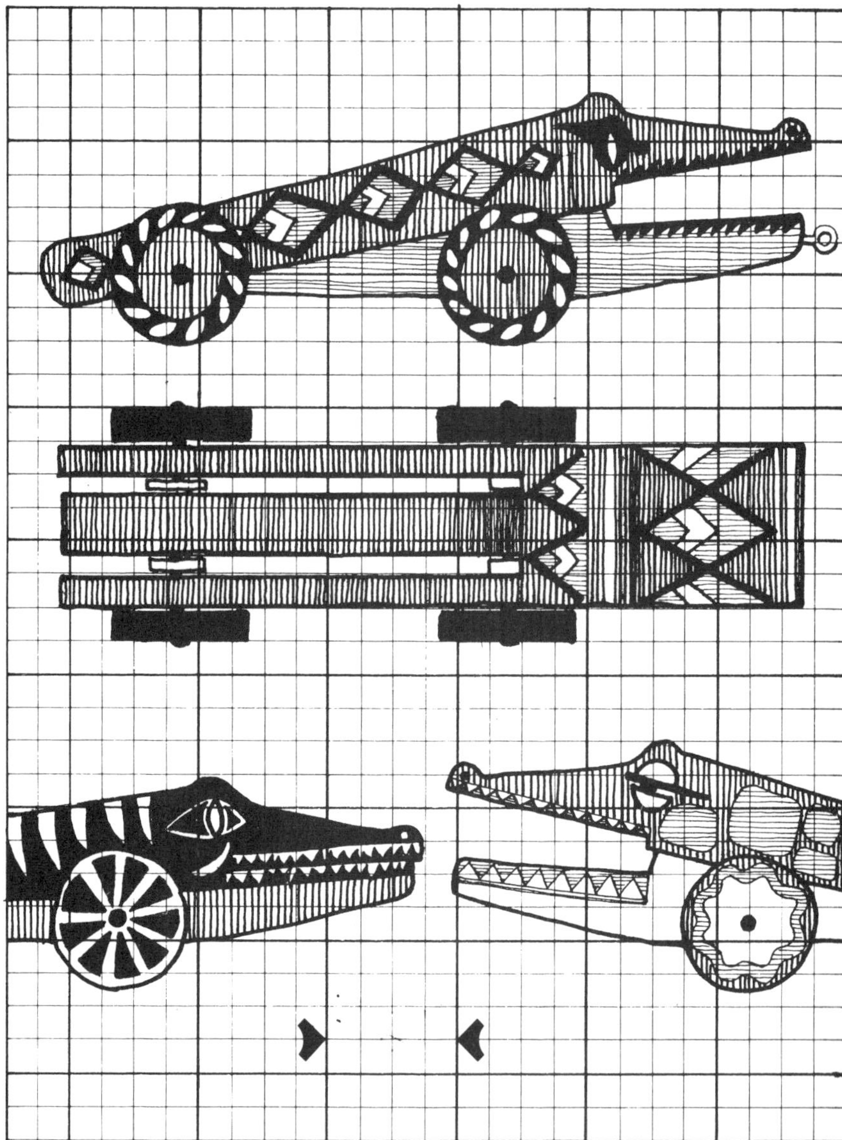

*Working Drawing, painting grid – note the scale of four squares to two inches. See how the croc might be painted in any number of ways.*

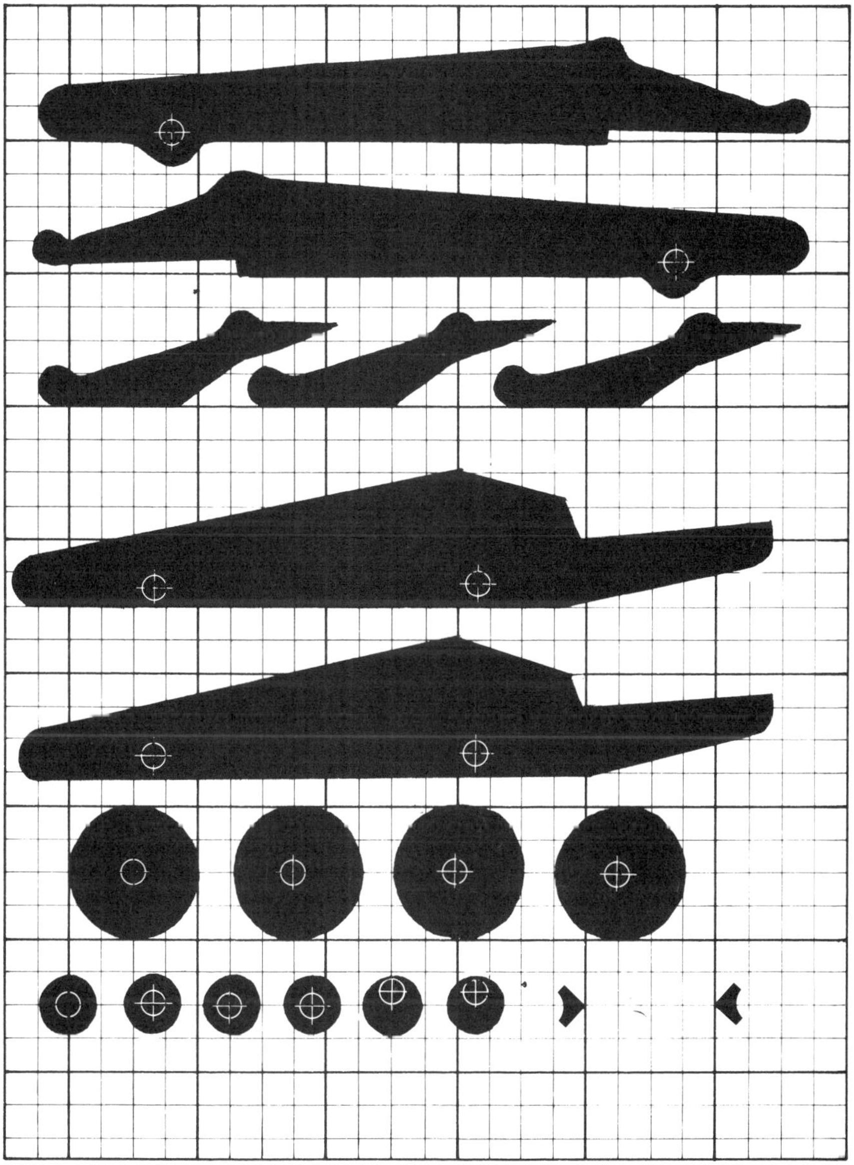

*Working Drawing, cutting grid – note the scale of four squares to two inches. There are seventeen cut-outs in all. See how two of the small discs are worked with off-centre holes and made into cams.*

fierce gnashing and clashing. Of course I thought of my toy as being unique, but not a bit of it; pull-along, wheeled, jaw-clacking toys have been around since Adam. There was little wooden mice with string operated jaws in ancient Egypt, there were wooden tigers with hinged jaws in Thebes, nineteenth century American whalers carved jaw-clacking scrimshaw whales, and so we could go on. We reckon that over the years, we've seen dozens of such toys: birds, rats, cats, fish, fowl and farm-yard animals. But best of all, we think, is a beautifully worked, museum-piece crocodile that was made over 3000 years ago in ancient Egypt. What pictures this little

Egyptian toy croc conjures up; we see a sort of technicolour scene complete with Pharaoh, palm trees, pyramids and Bible epic music, and right smack in the middle of our vision is an MGM type child playing with a jaw-clacking croc. Of course our fevered, Hollywood inspired imaginings are a million miles away from reality, but the ancient Egyptian toy is fact. We are comforted by the knowledge that if we or you took this croc out of his glass case and gave him to a twentieth century child, he would immediately be at home.

## CONSIDERING THE PROJECT

I would say that, of all the projects in this book, the 'Crunchy Croc' is at one and the same time the largest, the most complex, and the most difficult to put together. So, before you spend out and buy materials, or put tools to wood, take time and sit back with a measure and workout paper. Have a good long look at the working drawings and details, and note the complicated cam-operated jaw movement, and the placing of the various laminations, washers and dowels. See how the back axle is the pivotal point for the scissor-like upper jaws, and see also how the upper jaw side-plates rest on and are operated by the two front wheel cams. The jaw movement or sequence is — as the front wheel cams are on the up-turn, so the upper jaw is raised up, and as the cams go down, so the upper jaw clacks to rest on the lower.

It all sounds very complicated we know, but, like life, this project is simple enough to understand when you know how. It might help if we go through the project and tackle the problems a point at a time. The croc is made up from ¼ inch multiply, and the finished toy is about 12 inches long and 1¾ inches wide. There are seventeen ply cut-outs in all — two top body side-plates, two bottom body side-plates, three top jaw's spacers, four wheels, four washers and two cams. Note also the two 1¾–2 inch long, 3/16 inch diameter hardwood dowels.

Now, if you like the overall idea of the croc, but want to make him smaller, longer or whatever, then all well and good, but do bear in mind that the size, placing and profiles of both jaws, and their relationship to each other and the front wheel cams, are all critical. Take our advice, if you want to adjust, modify or in any way re-work the design, then you must make a full size prototype.

## MATERIALS

For this project you need a piece of white faced ¼ inch thick multiply that measures about 14×18 inches, five inches of 3/16 inch hardwood dowel, a small quantity of white PVA wood glue, a resin car body type filler, a stout brass screw eyelet, a yard or so of strong cord, a selection of model makers paints, and lastly you need a primer, an undercoat and brush cleaner.

**Tools** You need the use of a bench vice or worktable holdfast, a coping saw and a pack of spare blades, a hand drill with a 3/16 inch drill bit, a selection of stick-tools, a pack of graded sandpapers, a compass, a small sharp knife, a small wood rasp, a ruler, and finally you need a full range of small tools like pencils, workout paper and tracing paper.

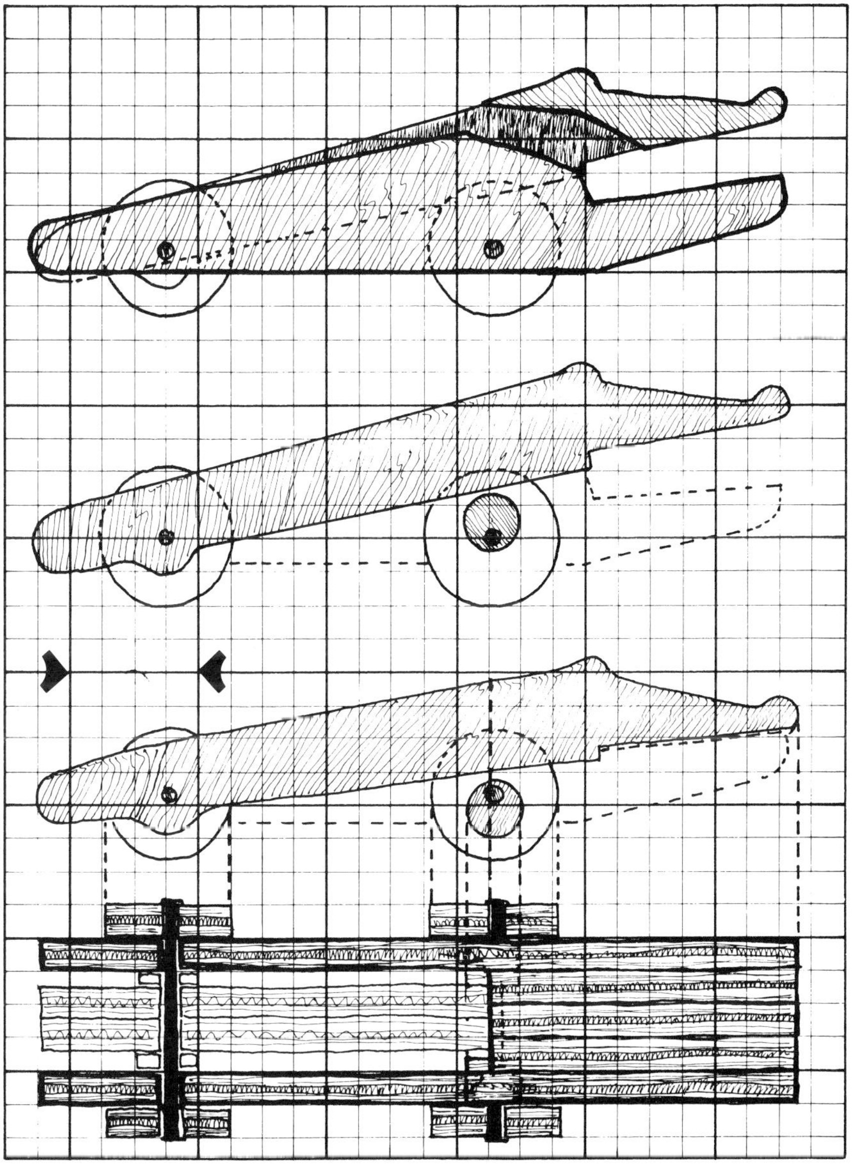

*Working Drawing, assembly grid – note the scale of four squares to two inches. Note how the front wheel cams raise and lower the upper jaw.*

## SETTING OUT THE DESIGN

First take your sheet of wood and check it over for such faults as cracks, stains and loose knots. Then take a sheet of gridded paper, and work the various shapes and profiles to size. Note the working drawing scale of four grid squares to two inches. This done, trace the master designs, then pencil press transfer the lines of the design through to the working face of the wood. Now go over the transferred lines with a soft pencil, and then label all the parts, that is to say – 'top jaw', 'spacers', 'wheels' and so on.

When you are sure that all is as it should be, take a pencil and very carefully establish the position of the sixteen pivotal holes: a back axle hole in each of the two upper side plates, two axle holes in each of the lower side-plates, a hole in each of the four wheels, a hole in each of the four washers, and finally an off-centre hole in each of the two cams.

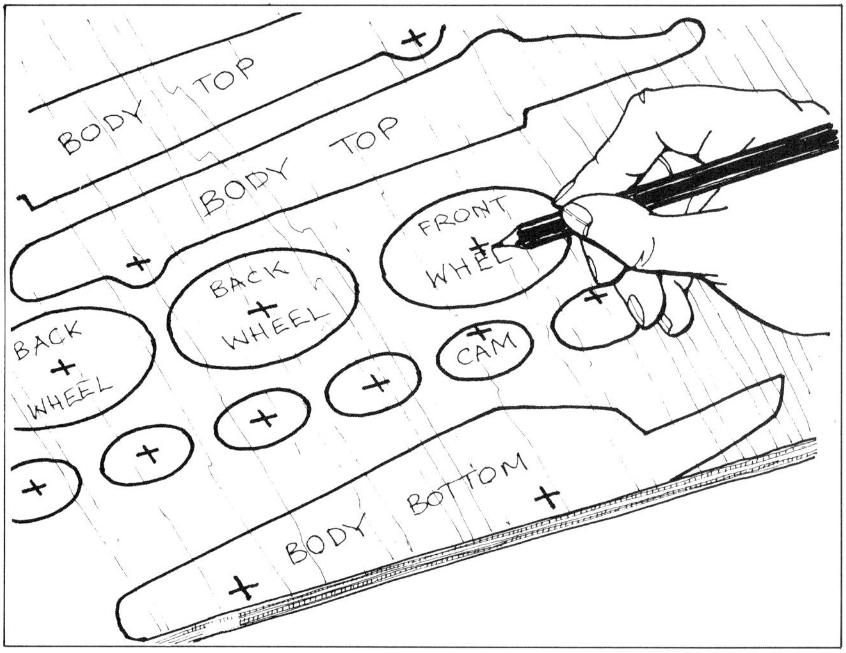


*Pencil press transfer the shapes to the wood, then re-work the lines and label the parts.*

## CUTTING AND GLUING

Put the wood in the clamp, or vice, take up the coping saw, then start to carefully cut out the drawn shapes. Work at it slowly — cut in from the edge of the wood, keep the saw blade at right angles to the working face of the ply, and keep the line of cut outside the drawn lines. And so you continue, until you have cut out all seventeen ply shapes.

This done, work the wood with rasp, knife and sandpaper, until the profiles are all crisp edged. Don't try, at this stage, for a perfect finish; just make sure that the rough sawn edges are free from burrs and splinters.

Now smear a little PVA glue on the various pieces of ply, as illustrated, and build up the two main toy part laminations. You should now have a ½ inch thick lower jaw/croc body, and a 1¼ inch thick upper jaw/croc body. Now being extra careful that you don't twist the gluey 'sandwiches' off true, place them in a clamp and leave them be for at least twenty-four hours.

## DRILLING AND RUBBING DOWN

When the glue is dry, take a pencil and carefully re-establish the position of the various pivotal points. Now support the ply with scrap wasters, or back boards, then work the $^{3}/_{16}$ inch holes.

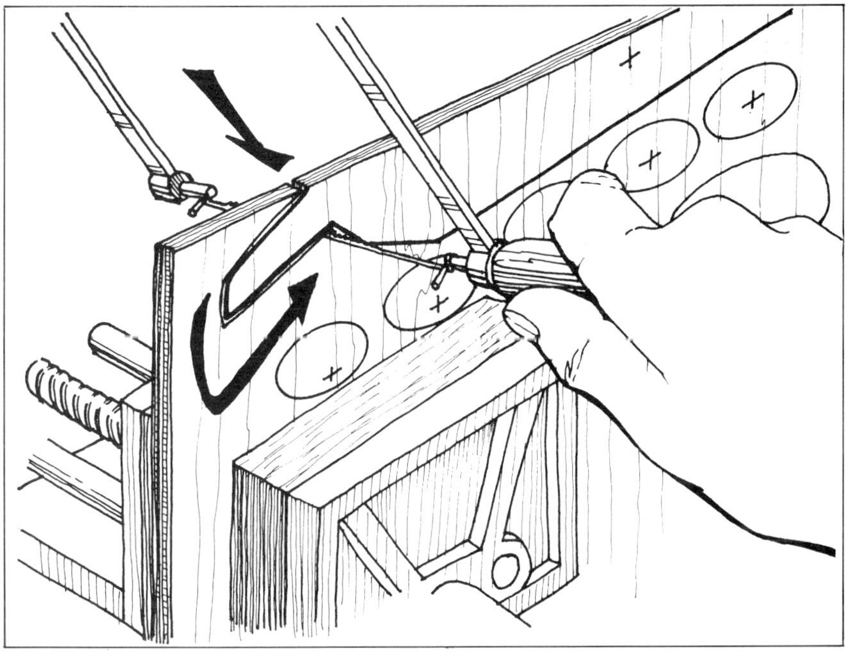

*Put the wood to be sawn in the vice, and then set-to with the coping saw. Keep the blade at right angles to the wood, and make sure that you cut on the outside of the drawn line.*

This done, have a trial putting together — place the upper croc jaw over the lower, check for alignment, position the washers and cams, push home the dowels, and set the wheels. At this stage, the cams will be loose on the axles, so the jaw raising won't occur; but no matter, you will be able to make sure

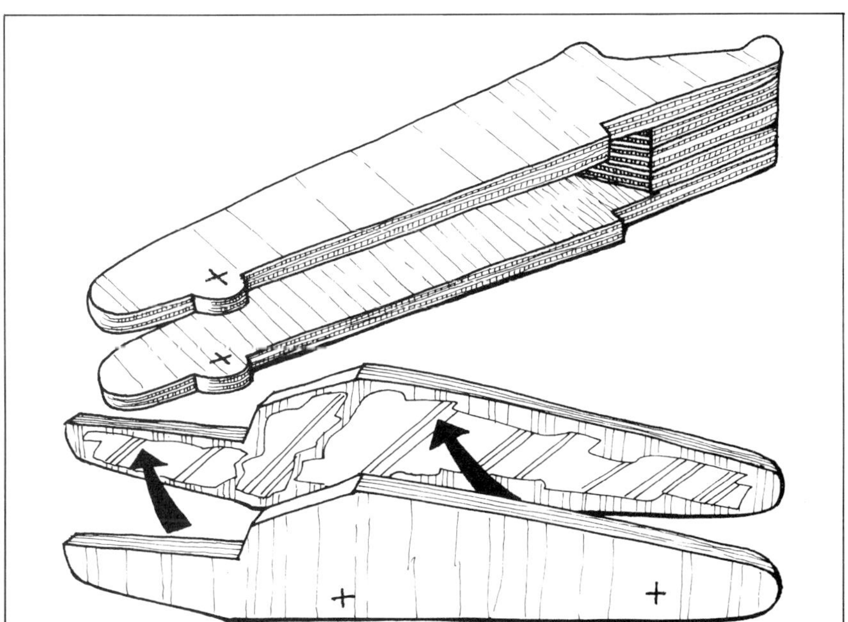

*Smear glue on the wood, and build up the two main croc body parts.*

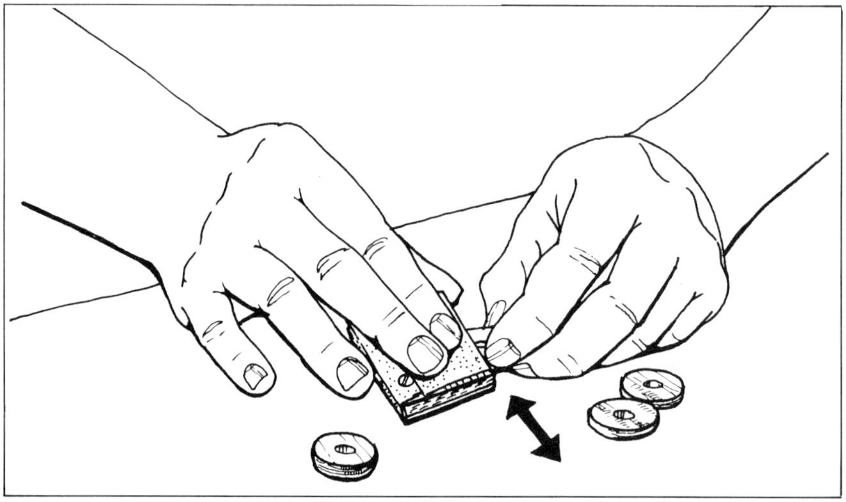

*Sand down the washers so that they are a good easy fit.*

that the jaws come together nicely, and the axles run straight. Note – for a perfect smooth-moving toy, it will be necessary to rub down the thickness of the washers – see the working drawings and details.

Now, when you are pleased with the overall fitting, strip the toy back down to its component parts, and then glue-fix the cams to the front wheels as shown. This done, mix a little resin filler and go over all the ply shapes, and make good any grain tears and cut-edge cavities. Finally, take your stick tools and graded sandpapers, and work all the wood to a smooth rounded finish.

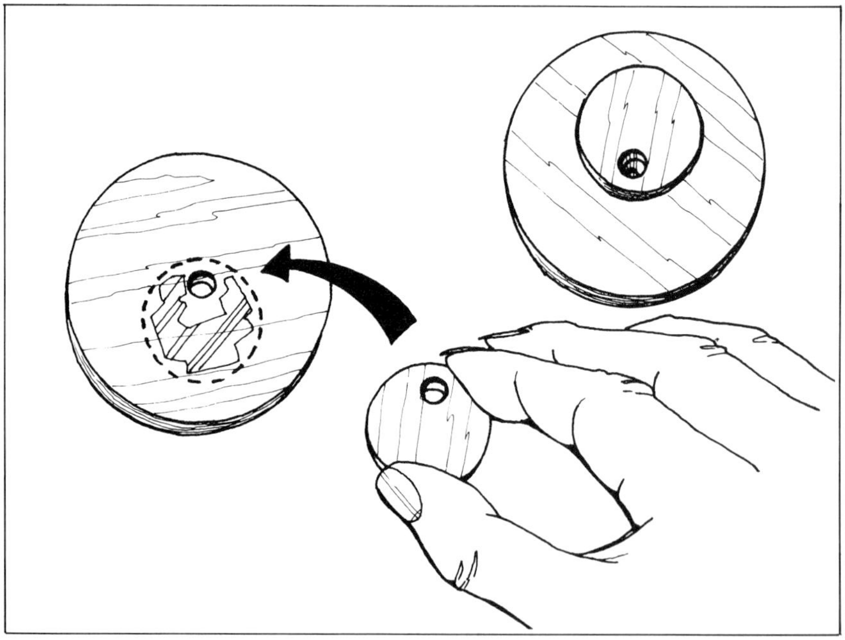

*Glue the cams, and place them on the front wheels. Note – it is important that the holes be well placed and aligned.*

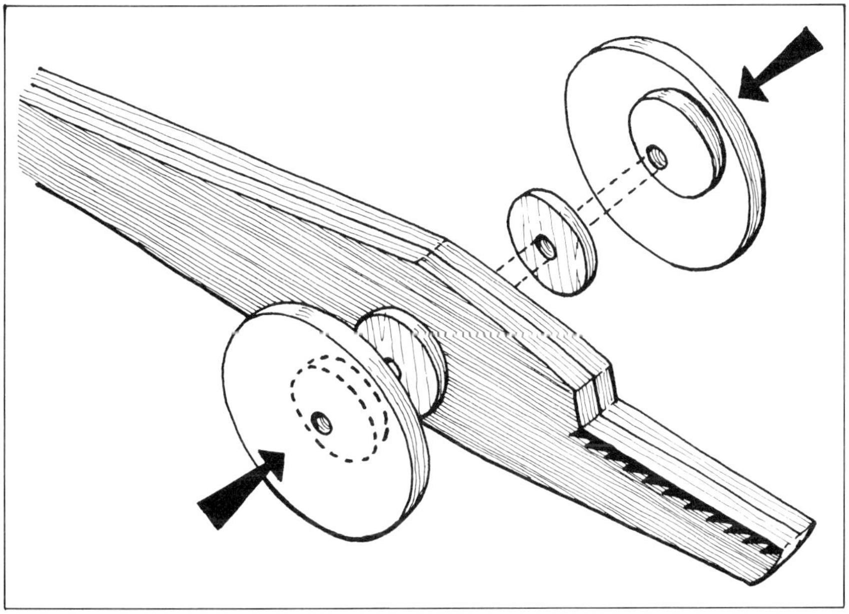

*When you come to gluing the front wheels on the axle dowel, make sure that the cams are matched.*

## PAINTING

Clear away all the bench clutter, arrange your brushes and paints, then set out all the prepared toy parts. You should now have two back wheels, two front wheels complete with aligned and glue-fixed cams, four washers, all worked to a good fit, a lower croc body with two axle holes, and lastly an upper croc body with back axle holes.

Now, checking with your colour design reference notes, and of course drying and rubbing down between coats, lay on a primer, an undercoat, and a smooth well finished topcoat.

Lastly, when the top ground coat is dry, take a fine-point brush, and with swift bold strokes, pick out the multicoloured details of the croc's body, face and wheel patterning.

Finally, take a scrap of sandpaper, and, when the paint is completely dry, clean out the croc body axle holes so that they are a loose fit for the $^3/_{16}$ inch dowel.

## PUTTING TOGETHER

Brush down the worksurface, spread out a clean cloth, say a piece of old sheeting, then set out the cut and painted ply, the hardwood dowels and the PVA glue. Now take the lower body and position the washers and the front wheels, as shown – that is to say in the side-to-side sequence; a cam-wheel with the cam on the inside, a washer, the 'two-thickness' croc body, another washer, and finally the other cam-wheel, again with the cam on the inside. This done, check that all the parts are aligned, then push home the axle dowel, dab a little PVA glue into the wheel holes, and lastly push on the wheels.

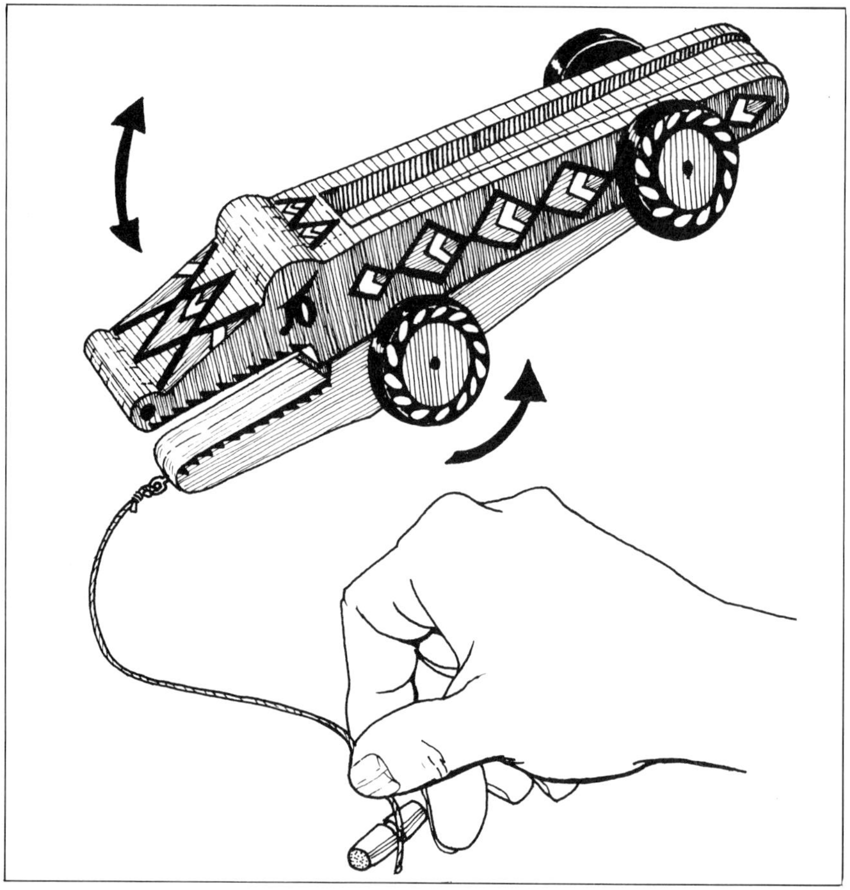

*In use, the croc is dragged around, the wheels turn, the cams go round and the jaws go up and down.*

Now place the croc on a smooth worksurface and find and mark the point on both cams that is furthest away from the axle. When you have marked the cams, place the croc at eye-level, and turn and adjust one or other of the wheels until the cams are identically matched, that is to say, they are both up, or both down.

This done, gently move the wheels and check that both cams rise and fall together. Finally, place the upper part of the croc over the lower, align the holes, push the axle into position, and then glue and fix the wheels. Now for the big test, place the croc on a level surface and slowly push him forward. If all's well, the axles will turn loosely in the body holes, the cams will rise and fall, and the croc jaws will snap up and down. When you are sure that the croc works as described, let the glue dry, then screw home the lower jaw brass eyelet, and knot-in the pull-along cord.

## AFTERTHOUGHTS

If the up-and-down, movement of the croc's jaw is to operate smoothly, the cams must be balanced so that on the 'up', they lift the jaw, and on the 'down' they lose contact with the jaw and leave it at rest on the lower jaw.

If, on completion, the cams don't quite lose contact with the upper side-plates, and so let the croc jaw snap shut, you might have to reduce the wood at the cams, or trim back the side-plates.

# BIBLIOGRAPHY


TOYS AND WHISTLES
Bailey, C. S. Published by Viking, 1937.

THE STREET MARKETS OF LONDON
Benedetta, Mary Published by John Miles, 1936.

MAKING NURSERY TOYS
Catford, Nancy Published by Muller, 1944.

GORDON CRAIG BOOK OF PENNY TOYS
Craig, Gordon Published London, 1899.

THE TOYS OF THE LITTLE FOLK OF ALL AGES AND COUNTRIES
Cremer, Henry Published London 1873.

NURSERY LIFE THREE HUNDRED YEARS AGO
Crump, Lucy Published by Routledge, 1929.

CHILDREN'S TOYS THROUGHOUT THE AGES
Daiken, Leslie Published by Batsford, 1953.

CHILD LIFE IN COLONIAL DAYS
Earle, A. M. Published USA, 1899.

THE ANCIENT WORLD
Glover, T. R. Published by Cambridge University Press, 1935 and Penguin, 1945.

PEEPSHOW INTO PARADISE: A HISTORY OF CHILDREN'S TOYS
Gordon, Lesley. Published by Harrap, 1953.

CHILDREN'S TOYS OF BYGONE DAYS
Grober, Carl Published by Batsford, 1932.

SIMPLE WOODEN TOYS
Haslam, Fred Published by Studio, 1945.

FOLKTOYS
Hercik, Emanuel Published by Orbis, 1951.

THE HANDBOOK OF OLD AMERICAN TOYS
Hertz, L. H. Published Mark Haber New York, 1947.

CHILDREN'S TOYS OF YESTERDAY
Holme, Geoffrey Published by Studio, 1932.

DOLLS THE WORLD OVER
Hooper, Elizabeth Published Baltimore 1939.

WOODEN TOY MAKING
Horton, F. M. Published by Dryad Press, 1936.

TOYS OF OTHER DAYS
Jackson, E. N. Published by Newnes, 1907.

TOYS, THEIR DESIGN AND CONSTRUCTION
Kay, J. & White, C. Published by University of London Press, 1944.

ENGLISH POPULAR AND TRADITIONAL ART
Lambert, M. and Marx, E. Published by Sterling, New York, 1985.

WOODWORK AND TOYMAKING
Richards, B. T. Published by Bell, 1950.

TOYS AND TOYMAKERS
Tippett, J. S. Published New York, 1931.

TOYS YOU CAN MAKE OF WOOD
Turpin, L. Published by Pitman 1947.

PENNY PLAIN, TWOPENCE COLOURED
Wilson, A. E. Published by Harrap, 1932.

# INDEX